"*Funny* in our day often means cynical. *Deep* often implies heavy and over my head. But Stephen James and David Thomas avoid those traps. They're funny beyond words and deep with an honesty that touches the heart without being sentimental. I love listening to them. *How to Hit a Curveball* is wildly funny and immensely true to the core of what it means to be a man. Suffering is not an option, but how we engage our struggles will define the kind of men we become."

Dan B. Allender, Ph.D.
president, Mars Hill Graduate School
author of *To Be Told* and *Leading with a Limp*

D1299143

Stephen James | David Thomas

HOW TO HIT A CURVE BALL
GRILL THE PERFECT STEAK
AND BECOME A REAL MAN

learning what our fathers never taught us

TYNDALE HOUSE PUBLISHERS, INC.
CAROL STREAM, ILLINOIS

Visit Tyndale's exciting Web site at www.tyndale.com

TYNDALE and Tyndale's quill logo are registered trademarks of Tyndale House Publishers, Inc.

How to Hit a Curveball, Grill the Perfect Steak, and Become a Real Man: Learning What Our Fathers Never Taught Us

Designed by Erik M. Peterson

Edited by Dave Lindstedt

Library of Congress Cataloging-in-Publication Data

James, Stephen.
   How to hit a curveball, grill the perfect steak, and become a real man : learning what our fathers never taught us / Stephen James and David Thomas.
      p. cm.
   Includes bibliographical references (p.   ).
   ISBN-13: 978-1-4143-1862-2 (sc)
    ISBN-10: 1-4143-1862-6 (sc)
   1. Men (Christian theology) 2. Christian men—Religious life. I. Thomas, David.
II. Title.
   BT703.5.J37 2008
   248.8'42—dc22   2008000836

TO OUR FATHERS

Thomas Neely James Jr.
and Monty Gene Thomas

FOR OUR SONS

Elijah, Henry, and Teddy James
and Baker and Witt Thomas

CONTENTS

Acknowledgments

Creating this book felt, at times, like being caught between a rock and a hard place. First, there was our writing deadline. The bulk of the manuscript was written during the summer months, sandwiched between May and September. It was kind of cramped. But the really tight spot was standing in the gap between our fathers and our sons. We're both fortunate to still have our fathers with us, and we are blessed to have sons of our own; yet it's an awkward place to be.

Much of who we are as men we can credit to our fathers. Much of who we long to be we can credit to our sons. In writing this book, we each gained a much deeper appreciation of our fathers' love, the struggle of being a man, and the challenge of raising boys. Thank you, Dads.

Our sons have exposed in us more than we ever could have imagined. More love, more passion, more fear, more futility, more incompetence, more hope, more faith, more laughs, more tears. You boys are already showing us glimpses of the great men you will one day become.

If anyone carried the burden of this book, it is our wives, not us. Heather and Connie, your support and permission (and sometimes sheer tolerance) of the writing process is humbling. Much of what we know of ourselves as men is directly related to what you have loved us into being. Our daughters, too, have revealed to us depths in our masculinity that we never knew existed—things like tenderness, wonder, stillness, and longing.

We also owe a debt of gratitude to our two agents, Matt Baugher and Greg Daniel. You are each wise men who serve and lead with humility and vision. Thank you both for sharing this burden with us.

We still can't believe that we get to work with such an incredible publishing company in Tyndale House Publishers. Our experience with y'all continues to be amazing. We consider you more than colleagues; you have become good friends (and great dinner companions). Our deep gratitude is extended to Ron Beers, Carol Traver, Kathy McClelland, Dave Lindstedt, Mavis Sanders, Keri Tryba, and Travis Thrasher.

Last, and certainly most importantly, we thank God. As men, we are continually awed and grateful that he has given us a platform to speak to his miraculous story. It is our prayer that he would continue to keep us humble and meet us on our journey toward authentic manhood.

If

Rudyard Kipling

If you can keep your head when all about you
Are losing theirs and blaming it on you;
If you can trust yourself when all men doubt you,
But make allowance for their doubting too;
If you can wait and not be tired by waiting,
Or being lied about, don't deal in lies,
Or being hated, don't give way to hating,
And yet don't look too good, nor talk too wise:

If you can dream—and not make dreams your master;
If you can think—and not make thoughts your aim;
If you can meet with Triumph and Disaster
And treat those two imposters just the same;
If you can bear to hear the truth you've spoken
Twisted by knaves to make a trap for fools,
Or watch the things you gave your life to, broken,
And stoop and build 'em up with worn-out tools;

If you can make one heap of all your winnings
And risk it on one turn of pitch-and-toss,
And lose, and start again at your beginnings
And never breathe a word about your loss;
If you can force your heart and nerve and sinew
To serve your turn long after they are gone,
And so hold on when there is nothing in you
Except the Will which says to them: "Hold on!"

If you can talk with crowds and keep your virtue,
Or walk with kings—nor lose the common touch,
If neither foes nor loving friends can hurt you,
If all men count with you, but none too much;
If you can fill the unforgiving minute
With sixty seconds' worth of distance run,
Yours is the Earth and everything that's in it,
And—which is more—you'll be a Man, my son!

Where I (Stephen) grew up, seventh grade was the first year we had our own lockers. They were the long, skinny kind and the color of urine.

That year, my locker was in the big hall that ran in front of the central office. It was like Main Street. The entrance to the school was right around the corner, and unless you were headed to Shop or P.E., you were walking right by my locker. Between classes, I went to my locker to swap out books, but it was really more of an opportunity to talk with friends and act goofy with the girls than anything else.

One day in February, a rumor started circulating that a girl named Jenny "liked" me and wanted to "go together." This news was both exciting and terrifying. I had never *gone* with anybody—heck, the only time I had even called a girl was once on an overnight at a friend's house, when we had prank-called a girl and hung up when she answered. I had heard from some of the more experienced guys that "going together" meant things like holding hands and kissing. And some guys even talked about getting to "second base," which I figured out had something to do with a different kind of curve than the ones I'd seen on a baseball field. This Jenny was really cute and was known to be somewhat aggressive in terms of "base running," which only served to heighten my anxiety.

By lunchtime, the gossip had spread through my social circle, and I was on the lookout for Jenny. I didn't know what I was going to say if I saw her, but I knew I had better think of something.

So there I was at my locker, swapping out books, when a friend of mine nudged me and said, "Hey, dude, here she comes." Out of the corner of my eye, I saw Jenny coming down the hall toward me, her shoulder-length blonde hair swaying from side to side in rhythm with her steps. I freaked out in fear and stared straight into my locker, hoping that she would just pass on by.

It is worth noting that in seventh grade I really wasn't very cool. I had the physique of a middle-aged man and the fashion sense of, well, a seventh-grade boy. Back then, I still feathered my hair back each morning with pride (kind of like Scott Baio on *Joanie Loves Chachi*—not at all like the more preppy Scott Baio on *Charles in Charge*), and on this particular day I was wearing a pale-gray Kmart sweatsuit with deep pockets.

I swear the hall grew quiet as Jenny drew closer. Everyone was waiting to see what would happen. I stood there, holding my books and praying, "God, please let this get over with quickly."

Then it happened.

I felt a tug at my pants, and the next thing I knew, I was blowing in the wind—all of me.

You see, in an attempt to embarrass me by pulling down my sweatpants, Jenny had *also* gotten ahold of my tighty-whities and exposed me, in all my prepubescent glory, to the entire school.

For an instant, I stood frozen, with my arms full of books, my heart pounding in shame, and a cold breeze blowing between my legs. Then I dropped the books and grabbed at my pants, but not before I had earned a list of nicknames, including Winnie the Pooh, Mooner, Crack Attack, Chief Pale Cheeks, and the one that would stick with me the rest of the year: Flash. It stuck so well that people even signed my yearbook "To Flash" later that spring when school let out.

Funny now, but it wasn't funny then. It was one of those moments where I learned a tough lesson about how painfully exposing life can be.

Sadly, the shame I felt that day is not terribly unique. What guy hasn't been knocked around by life? What guy hasn't been exposed as insufficient or inept?

Remember Little League? The evening breeze heavy with the scent of honeysuckle; the crowd of anxious parents cheering; the *ting* of aluminum bats; and the lump filling your throat as you dug into the batter's box, silently begging the pitcher, *Please, please don't throw me a curveball.*

Remember sneaking behind the bleachers with a *real* girl, a girl that smelled like green apples and roses; anxiously fumbling with your words and the awkward silences; leaning toward her, your eyes half-closed and your heart thumping, paralyzed with wonder at that first soft touch of her lips. Your heart enraptured with the delight of first love . . . until a few weeks later when she dumped you for the new kid in town.

And let's not forget car trouble. Driving down the road when your car starts sputtering, wheezing, and spewing. You coax it into the nearest service station, where a grease-stained guy named Bubba greets you, pops the hood, and smugly asks, "What seems to be the trouble?" And you have no idea.

Something's Starting to Stink

Moments like these begin to stack up in a guy's life like manure in a horse stall. Let's be really honest here: No guy makes it past seventeen or eighteen without receiving his fair share of dings to his manhood—and that's if he's lucky. By the time most guys get their driver's license, they have already experienced enough emotional and spiritual fender benders that their hearts are dented and their self-image is scratched for years to come.

You know what we're talking about: parents divorcing, grandparents dying, being shamed by a coach or mentor, being rejected by a girl, humiliating yourself in front of a crowd, being betrayed by someone you trusted, or having your hopes and dreams evaporate like spilled gasoline.

Everybody gets kicked a few times in life. That's a given. The only question is *where* have you been kicked (teeth, guts, nuts, shins) and *who* did the kicking (friend, foe, family, God). Heartache is not terribly diverse, but it's certainly widespread. As counselors, we've heard thousands of sad stories from men. Every man loses his innocence at some point—some of us gradually, and some more suddenly.

Sadly, these assaults to the masculine heart result in far more than adolescent angst. When a guy's heart has been wounded, the results are significant: self-protection, distrust of others, suspicion of God, and a fervent reliance on the four horsemen of self-sufficiency: training, talent, willpower, and intellect.

Once wounded by life, most guys come to depend

far more deeply on their own skills, aptitudes, resolve, strength, and brains than they do on God. They build facades that hide the truth of who they really are. These facades come in all shapes, sizes, and combinations. They can be tough, cold, or calculating; childish, whimsical, or charming; powerful, aggressive, or assertive; pious, intellectual, or contemplative; conservative, radical, or compassionate. You get the idea. In short, we learn to fake it.

Life is painful. Though we all experience seasons of happiness, life in this world is mostly defined by loss, difficulty, and struggle. No matter our skill set, intellect, creativity, personality, or faithfulness, we cannot escape the heartache that comes with living in a wrecked world that is groaning to be repaired.[1] For men, this reality is uniquely hard to bear and can be even harder to articulate.

There is a myth that much of contemporary Christianity has bought into: If you *do* it right, *think* about it right, *pray* about it right, and *try* hard enough, then your life will be successful and you will be "blessed." You know what? That's really much more than a myth. It's a propaganda campaign, a deception, straight from the pit of hell.

Unfortunately, men are especially susceptible to this line of heresy. Too often, in response to our heartache, self-doubt, or mistrust, we buy into a philosophy that suggests we can escape the pain, incompetence, and futility that is so common to life. It's tempting to adopt an attitude that says, "If we focus enough on our families, keep the right promises, and fill our toolboxes with the correct gear, then we, too, can win at work and at home." What guy doesn't love a quick fix? We're all about finding a definitive solution.

There are some very successful and popular Christian organizations (parachurch ministries, publishing houses, megachurches, and denominations) whose primary work is to sell this snake oil of self-performance. They spend much of their time promoting an ideology that says, "If you want to prosper and you want your life to turn out okay, then all you need is to do the *right* thing, the *right* way, at the *right* time." The problem with this way of thinking is that it is contrary to what the Bible teaches, and it doesn't square with the reality of life.

We're All Losers . . . and Winners

Productivity and competency are not essential for living fully as a man. One treasured gift that authentic Christianity affords to guys who accept it is that we are free to live without weight and pressure. We don't have to try to earn our worth through what we make of our lives. In fact, full living becomes possible only when we recognize our powerlessness and surrender to God. That's the threshold of freedom and the beginning of authentic manhood. If a man is fortunate enough to enter into reconciliation with God, he can be liberated from the prison of performance.[2]

Christian spirituality offers men a way out of the traps of relying on our abilities and accomplishments. Whether we are goofballs or sages, screwups or tycoons, bums or ne'er-do-wells. Whether we clear the bar or not, our manhood is determined by the content of our hearts, not the plaques on the wall, the size of our wallets, or even the goodness of our families.[3] Authentic manhood is about living from the heart with integrity, passion, and intimacy.

Any guy who has stayed awake for ten minutes in church could probably tell you that there is a big difference between knowing something in your head and having an experience in your heart that changes who you are.

What if being an authentic man has nothing to do with building a successful career, having a nice family, or mastering the mechanics of daily life? What if authenticity has far more to do with courageously tackling the deep questions of the heart, struggling with yourself and with God, and finding out who you are really made to be?

We guys have learned from an early age how to squash our hearts and hide who we really are. Yet we desperately want to be known. The trouble comes in that we're also afraid to reveal our hearts to those who might judge us or reject us. Erwin McManus articulates this well:

> We're all struggling to figure ourselves out. We're afraid to expose our souls to those who might judge us, and at the same time, we desperately need help to guide us on this journey. If we're not careful, we might find ourselves with everything this world has to offer and later find we have lost ourselves in the clutter.[4]

We've gotten really good at endeavoring toward *mastery* as a way of escaping life's hard knocks and compensating for our inherent shortcomings.

But here's the truth: No matter what kind of home you've come from, there are things your father didn't teach you, lessons you didn't learn, and questions you never had answered. Whether your dad was an all-star or a strikeout, one thing is for sure: He wasn't perfect. There were holes in his game. He didn't give you everything you needed.

Why This Book?

So why another book for men? Good question. For me (David), the answer came on a Monday night when I was teaching a class I've offered for years called Nurturing Boys. The class is designed for parents, mentors, coaches, educators, or anybody who cares about boys. We spend three weeks wrestling with understanding boys: who they are, what they need, how they learn, and what they want. I address topics ranging from organized sports to wet dreams, video games to dating, academics to pornography, and everything in between.

In the class, I teach a section on what a boy needs from a mom and what a boy needs from a dad. In instructing fathers, one point of discussion is the importance of having an *ongoing* dialogue (not a onetime "birds and bees" talk) about development, sexuality, and the changes that take place for a young man during puberty. Every time I've taught this class over the past decade, every man in the room looks at me like I'm asking him to teach his son needlepoint while speaking Japanese. If it weren't so tragic to see their expressions, it would be comical. It's a room full of deer in the headlights.

Where does their panic come from? As I've talked with these guys, I've learned that they all lack adequate role models in this area. They have no point of reference. I've yet to meet a man whose father had enough authentic conversations with him during his developmental years that he felt educated, informed, prepared, and confident about the changes to come. And because they have no personal experience on which to draw, the idea of engaging their own sons in this kind of dialogue feels like driving cross-country without a road map or a GPS. It just won't happen.

Usually, I attempt to defuse the panic with some humor. I say to the guys, "Well, obviously we all got the information somehow. We all managed to procreate, didn't we? We figured out that *this* part must fit inside *this* part." I typically find that most men came by the information through some risky means, or else they just stumbled into it when they got married. They either overheard some guys talking in the locker room (miseducation), discovered pornography (pollution), figured it all out through experimentation with themselves and with the opposite sex (trial and error), or some combination of the above. But more often than not, their fathers failed to initiate them into manhood with accurate information, useful instruction, or engaging leadership.

Even if you are one of the rare guys whose dad did try to instruct you, it's still likely he didn't give you all that you needed. He fell short of being perfect and was likely not as present as you needed him to be. Or he was, and then he wasn't.

I've heard stories ranging from that of a friend whose dad trapped him in the car on an out-of-town trip and forced him to sit in silence for five hours listening to cassette tapes about adolescence and sexuality, to a client whose mom showed him illustrations of erect penises and talked about how masturbation could cause him to develop permanent genital warts. (And then, when he came out of his room, his dad said, "So you got it now? You have any questions about all that stuff your mother just told ya?") These tragedies are only a couple of examples of guys who didn't get what they so desperately needed.

And learning about our bodies is just one small piece of it. There's so much more—from car care to dating to parenting to teamwork to spirituality to finances to you name it. No dad could give us everything we need. And even if he tried, he would likely step on our toes in the process. As dads now ourselves, we're already experiencing bumps in the road with our own sons. It's like the harder we try to get it right, the more we mess it up along the way.

But that doesn't mean there's no hope. In fact, that's why we wrote this book. You see, even though we're all working with broken pieces (which is a product of the Fall, let alone our own family histories), we can come to grips with our brokenness and begin to be restored to what God designed for us to be.

Wanted: Instruction Manual for Life

In our culture, most boys make the journey to manhood without a clear vision for what a man is designed to be. There are lessons and skills that we needed and never learned. As adults now, a lot of us have had to go looking for things to fill in the gaps. Sometimes we fill the gaps with good things. And sometimes we don't.

If your dad never gave you the information you needed, if you missed the instruction, if you've felt unprepared and incompetent at various points in your journey as a man—congratulations, you're normal. Every guy feels unequipped and underprepared at some level. It's not like there's an instruction manual with step-by-step procedures for every possible situation. In fact, what we really needed to learn from our fathers is how to recover when life throws us something unexpected. When we're sitting on the fastball and get the curve—or a knuckleball—instead. Part of what it means to be a man is learning how to adapt and how to bring order out of chaos.

In the next seven chapters, we will talk to you honestly about what it means to be a man. We'll tell you some of the things your dad never told you—and maybe a few he did, and we'll share some things we've learned along the way. Even if your dad was incredible, even if he was well-intentioned and purposeful, he probably skipped over some information that would have proven useful to you in your journey of becoming a man.

This book is centered on seven core experiences that many guys face. By looking closer at these experiences, we will see how there is a deeper (and often humorous) reality at play. If men can discover more deeply the questions that stir in their hearts and then begin to address them, they can begin to be more invested in their passions, their families, their God, and their lives.

By inviting you to engage in the process and exploring some of the roadblocks we encounter along the way, we will address the basic issues that all men experience. In doing so, we hope you will begin to come to grips with your own story. And we hope that along the way you will find some other guys to share your stories with. (And if you are married we hope you will share them with your wife.) And if you have a son or know a son who needs a dad, we hope that you will share these stories with him, too. He needs to hear them as much as you need to tell them—especially the hard ones.

Who Wrote This Book

First and foremost, we're guys who are on our own journeys. We know from our own experience that being a real man is easier said than done. Part of this book is us candidly revealing our own successes and failures as men, sons, and fathers. We are also therapists. Every day, we use our training and experiences to help men and boys, and the women who love them, journey further into their own hearts so that they can be more of who they were made by God to be.

We'll also speak of places where our dads disappointed us and failed to give us some of the information we so desperately needed and desired. Equally, we will speak to some of the extraordinary things they offered to us.

So, we'll speak out of our own experience as men, fathers, sons, husbands, and therapists. We'll offer up some practical (and sometimes humorous) topics ranging from grilling a perfect steak to negotiating a raise, skinning a deer to perfecting the swan dive. There are sidebars throughout the book that offer instruction on some basic "man friendly" practices.

More importantly, we'll offer our two cents on some deeper topics like the art of authentic manhood, engaging the fairer sex, how to navigate male friendships, and the practice of leadership. Overall we have tried to bring an honest, entertaining, and helpful perspective that will illuminate the inner lives of men. So, head to the toilet (because that's where most men do their reading), and let's start the journey.

CHAPTER 1

How to Hit a Curveball

The Art of Authentic Manhood

In the spring of 1984, I (Stephen) was a fifth grader, and I was not cool.

In fact, on the social hierarchy, I was somewhere just below average and just above dork. I wasn't shunned or disliked, but neither was I popular. I was mostly ignored. I was vanilla ice cream. Sure, everybody likes vanilla ice cream. It's just not what most people would pick given the choice at Baskin-Robbins.

I did not, in any way, enjoy fifth grade. Hindsight being what it is, I can see now that I did have some good times, but with all things being equal, for me fifth grade sucked like a Hoover.

Earlier that year, my family had moved from my middle-class boyhood home out by the airport to a house on a hill in an upscale suburb south of town. What was a great move for my family was a bad move for me. The transition was horrible—kind of like drinking orange juice after brushing your teeth.

We moved from a neighborhood where I had friends in almost every house to a subdivision with only two kids my age. One was a girl, and the other was a guy who had hit puberty somewhere around kindergarten. (I called him Man-boy, though not to his face.) When I met him, he was already almost six feet tall.

Needless to say, I had trouble making new friends. Being a redneck in a community of white collars didn't help, either. In a culture of BMWs and Mercedes, my family was a nice Buick, and I came fully loaded with bright orange hair parted down the middle and feathered back on the sides—that's right, a flaming butt cut. It was a tragic scene.

The one place where I did meet some kids with whom I was able to build friendships was through the local sports leagues. Team sports became my sanctuary from the loneliness, shame, and awkwardness of school. I played soccer in the fall, basketball in the winter, and soccer again in the early spring. Slowly, I began to make connections.

When soccer was finished that spring, the father of a kid from my team invited me to come out for the local baseball league. "Absolutely!" I loved baseball. I had started playing tee-ball when I was three or four and had progressed up through coach pitch. I wasn't half bad, either. I was a good little infielder and could be counted on to put the bat on the ball. So, on a cold Saturday in April, I showed up at the ballpark for try-outs, along with a few hundred other boys from four to fourteen.

At the tryouts, we each hit a few balls, fielded a few grounders, caught a few flies, and ran the bases, while a line of dads watched with clipboards and rated our performances so they would know where to put us in the draft. The soccer dad ended up picking me for his eleven- and twelve-year-old team, and I was the young-est player on the team.

The first practice went well. I was enthusiastic and a hard worker, and when the first scrimmage came around, I found myself playing second base and bat-ting third.

Summer was just around the corner, I was playing baseball, I had made a few friends, and school was nearly over for the year. I was beginning to believe that fifth grade might turn out okay after all.

At the last practice before the first game, the coach handed out the uniforms. He gave them out by size, moving from largest to smallest. Being the youngest, I got my uniform last, and the wait about killed me. Those few minutes seemed like forever. Our uniforms were black and yellow, 100 percent polyester, with a silk-screen logo on the front (some insurance company, if I remember). After some final instructions about the upcoming game and the opening-day ceremonies, I raced excitedly to my mother, who was waiting for me in the parking lot.

The moment I got home, I ran to my bedroom to put on the uniform—stirrup socks and all. As kids, we are really cool that way. Our hopes, passions, and dreams unregulated. Our hearts right up against our rib cages. As I got dressed, I thought about Mickey Mantle, my favorite baseball player. He was tough as nails—a real man's man. His nickname said it all: Blood and Guts. *That's me,* I said to myself. *Blood and Guts.*

Fully outfitted, I walked into the bathroom to check out my uniform. When I climbed up onto the toilet to get a full view of myself in the mirror, my heart dropped. The uniform was way too small. I looked ridiculous—more like Fat Elvis than Mean Mickey. "Guts" was right. My pants were way too tight, and the shirt hugged my prepubescent, pudgy stomach so that I looked like John Goodman at an all-you-can-eat buffet.

I pulled at my shirt, trying to stretch it out, but to my chagrin, I learned my first lesson about polyester: It ain't cotton. In an instant, I went from sky-high to in the dumps. As I slinked down from the toilet, I tried to pep myself up. "You can still play baseball," I told myself in a weak attempt to manufacture a morsel of self-esteem.

The first game came, and we were the home team. When we took the field for warm-ups, I jogged out to my position between first and second base. But I was so self-conscious about my uniform that I might as well have been naked. Once the game began, I loosened up. I got a couple of hits and fielded a few balls, and when the game was over, I walked off the field feeling okay about myself. For the next few games, things progressed well.

By the sixth game of the season, I had nearly forgotten about my uniform issue. I was playing great, and my team was doing well. On this particular evening, we were the away team, so we batted first. On the mound against us was Man-boy—the kid from my neighborhood—all six-feet-tall, hairy-lipped inch of him.

The first two batters went down on three pitches each. With two outs, I approached the plate, determined to get something going. I knocked the dirt off my cleats and looked up at Man-boy standing on the mound. He looked even bigger than usual. My courage and resolve vanished in an instant. I got the feeling I needed to pee.

I was pretty sure that everybody could tell I was scared. For sure my coach could tell, because he yelled,

"Time!" and called me over for a chat. We met about halfway between third and home. "Stephen," he said sternly, "move back in the box, choke up a little on the bat, and wait on the fastball. Take a good, level swing."

"Yes, sir," I said, never taking my eyes off Man-boy. I made my way back to the plate, dug in my cleats, and got ready to hit. In a blur, the ball zoomed past me. I barely even saw it.

"Strike!" called the umpire.

I took a couple of practice swings. Man-boy went into his windup, reared back, and threw. Then I saw something amazing, something I had never seen before in my young baseball career. The ball started behind me, and then it came right at me. I turned my head, closed my eyes, and cringed before I heard the *pop* of the ball hitting the catcher's mitt.

"Ball," yelled the ump.

What was that? I was baffled. I was sure that pitch was going to hit me, but it hadn't. Again, my coach called a time-out. Again, we met along the third-base line. "That last pitch was a curveball," he said. "Don't worry, son. Just watch the ball and take a good swing. If it's another curve, don't swing. He can't throw it for a strike."

HOW TO HIT A CURVEBALL

It's been said that the quickest way to get from point A to point B is a straight line. But somewhere along the way, baseball pitchers figured out that the quickest way to sit a batter down is by putting a little *bend* in the ball. A good curveball can make even the best hitter look silly if he's not expecting it. Mastering the art of hitting a curveball is one of those things that separate the men from the boys.

According to former big leaguer and coach Rob Ellis, who has put together several training videos, here's what Hank Aaron had to say about it: "I can wait on the curveball because I know the pitcher can't throw the fastball by me."

Well, that worked great for Hammerin' Hank, but what about the rest of us? If you want to hit a breaking ball, here are a few things to remember:

1. **READ THE SPIN.** This is easier said than done when the ball is coming at you at eighty-plus miles per hour, but the best hitters claim to be able to read the spin on a curveball and distinguish it from a fastball.

2. **LIGHTEN UP.** Use a bat that's light enough that you can get around on a pitch, even if you've been fooled.

3. **BE PATIENT.** Keep your weight back and wait as long as possible before swinging.

4. **READ THE BREAK.** If it starts low, let it go. If it starts to hang, give it a bang.

5. **GO THE OPPOSITE WAY.** Instead of trying to pull the ball, hit it to the opposite field. Right-handed batters facing a right-handed pitcher should try to hit a curveball to right field.

6. **PRACTICE MAKES PERFECT.** Visit the local batting cage for a couple of weeks. Work on your timing, patience, and swing.

I got back in the batter's box, knocked the dirt off my cleats again, touched my bat to the outside corner of the plate, and waited.

Fastball.

I swung hard and foul tipped the pitch into the chain-link backstop.

"One ball! Two strikes!" The umpire declared. *All right!* I thought to myself. *I can do this.* The next pitch was another curve. Like the first one, this pitch seemed as if it started out behind me, and then came right at my head. I waited and held my ground. But this time there was no *pop* of the catcher's mitt. Only the muffled *thump* of the ball hitting me square in the back as I tried too late to get out of the way. Man, that hurt. As I shuffled to first base, I tried to choke back the tears of fear and pain and embarrassment.

My next time up, I got hit again. In fact, the same scene repeated itself on all three of my plate appearances.

Thump.

Thump.

Thump.

I was a magnet for Man-boy's errant curveball.

After that game, I was never the same. Over the course of the next couple of outings, I became frozen in the batter's box—watching pitch after pitch glide right by me. When I did take a swing, I did so with my eyes closed, more wishing than swinging. If I got on base, it was because of walks. Teams we played began to yell, "Easy out!" whenever I came to the plate. I was locked up in fear and shame, and in the field I began to commit errors because of it.

I ended the season as a late-inning substitute, batting last in the lineup and playing in the outfield. By the final game, I found myself alone in right field—the position of losers and dweebs. We were winning by three runs, so the coach figured it was safe to leave me in. I had been in the game for three innings, and not a single ball had made it out of the infield.

I remember kicking the ground and digging at a hole in the grass with my cleats. Then the tide of the game began to change. Our pitcher walked two batters and gave up a single down the third-base line. The bases were loaded now, and the winning run was at the plate. I remember praying, "Please, God, don't let him hit the ball to me."

The next batter fouled off pitch after pitch in an epic battle. It was a long at bat, made even longer by my paralyzing fear. I ran every possible scenario through my head of what could happen if the ball was hit to me. I was rattled with questions like, *What if I can't catch it? What if it's right to me and I drop the ball?* I began to formulate a plan for how I would run toward the ball and then accidently slip in the grass and fall so that I wouldn't have to try to make a play.

I don't remember how the game ended. But I do know that somewhere in right field that summer I promised myself I wouldn't let someone else's taunting hurt me again. I began to erect a wall around my heart.

I will never forget the heartache of fifth-grade Little League. That was the last year I played baseball.

When I think about that time, the first image that comes to mind is that of a pudgy, preadolescent boy with a butt cut, in a way-too-tight polyester baseball uniform. That picture about sums up my entire fifth-grade experience. What an icon of self-contempt. Over the course of the year, I lost most of my self-confidence, and along with it, much of my heart. The seeds of self-doubt had taken root, and I was beginning to grow ashamed of myself. I doubted that I would ever grow up to be a "real man."

"Real Man"

The traditional American view of a "real man" is a guy who is more like Dirty Harry or John Wayne than Frasier Crane or Fred Rogers. You know the guy: broad-shouldered, self-confident, rough, tough, and successful. The good news is that the rugged stereotype of an unemotional, power-hungry man is starting to fade in our society, and we are beginning to understand what a real man is supposed to look like. In Christian circles, we've been trying to come up with the answer for some time now. We've had Promise Keepers rallies, Family Life weekends, and Wild at Heart retreats.

All kinds of definitions are floating around Christendom about what it means to be a real man. They range from the really foundational, like Donald Miller's straightforward definition in *To Own a Dragon,* in which he points out that the only qualification for being a real man is having a penis.[1] (Brilliant!) And then there are the really expansive definitions, like Stu Weber's in his popular book *Tender Warrior,* in which he suggests that a real man has a vision, has a good family, reads the Bible, is consistent, has feelings, is kind, is caring, is helpful, and doesn't run from problems.[2] (Whew! That's a lot to juggle.)

Both of these definitions seem accurate—depending on your definition of *real.* If by "real" you mean what makes a man a man, then Donald Miller is right on. On the other hand, if what you mean by "real" is what a man is capable of becoming, then you might tend to migrate toward Stu Weber's definition, or other definitions and insights offered by writers such as Richard Rohr, John

Eldredge, Gordon Dalbey, Stephen Arterburn, Robert Lewis, and countless others.

So what's the deal? Why is there such a market for all this conversation about being a "real man"? Why is the need to feel *real* so prevalent? Why are so many guys struggling with the concept of masculinity?

One big reason is that no one (except Jesus) has ever gotten it completely right—and no one ever will. We all fail as men. We all fall short of perfection . . . way short . . . helplessly short.

Our own fathers—and their fathers before them— were no exception to this truth. At some point, every father drops the ball with his son. From a human perspective, there is no perfect dad. No father does it well enough to get us through childhood with our entire hearts intact.

Our fathers' imperfections, and how those have played themselves out in our lives, are a big deal. Guys who grew up in a home where their father was absent will often face serious ramifications. How your own father may have abandoned you through his lack of heart, knowledge, passion, wisdom, skill, presence, or willingness goes a long way toward defining your idea of manhood.

For guys whose fathers misused power and authority or were abusive in their efforts to control, train, discipline,

HOW TO SHAVE

Even if you choose to buy an electric razor, there may still be an occasion when you'll need to shave the old-fashioned way. (Your razor might die on the morning of a big presentation, you might travel to Prague and find that your hotel room has those funky European outlets, or you might decide one day that you'd like a really close shave.) So let's talk about shaving the way it should be done—with an old-fashioned, double-edge blade and a mugful of shaving cream—so that your face will be as smooth as a baby's bum.

1. **GET A WET SHAVE.** Always shave either in the shower or right after taking a shower. The hot water will soften your beard and the steam will open your pores (which in turn will cause your whiskers to rise). If you can't get a shower first, wash your face with hot water. Run hot water over your razor, too, so that the blade will be hot.

2. **USE SHAVING SOAP.** We're not talking about the stuff in a can; we're talking about the classic stuff that comes in a bar. Applying shaving soap is best accomplished with a badger-hair brush (not boar hair, which is pricklier), which further

preps the beard by raising the hairs and transferring water to the skin. Wet the brush and use it to whip the soap into a lather; then spread it on in a circular motion. Soaps made of glycerin are the best.

3. **SHAVE WITH THE GRAIN.** If you move the razor with the grain (in the same direction that your whiskers grow), you'll get a close shave without irritation. One sure way to irritate your skin and get ingrown hairs is by shaving "up," against the grain. Use long, even strokes, and rinse the blade between each stroke.

4. **RINSE AND REPAIR.** Shaving is traumatic to your skin, so post-shave care is needed. Rinse your face with cold water (to close the pores) and gently pat your face dry with a clean towel. Finish up with a good non-alcohol-based aftershave or moisturizer (preferably with sunblock).

Adapted from Corey Greenberg, "How to Get that Perfect Shave: Latest trends and products to avoid those nicks and cuts," www. msnbc.msn.com/id/6886845; and "The Perfect Shave," men. style.com/details/features/landing?id=content_5664.

or lead their sons, coming to terms with the impact of their father's harm is an important part of growing into their masculinity. How our dads may have shamed, controlled, or abused us through their misuse of power sets us up for misunderstanding our identity as men.

What Ifs?

What if the practice of becoming a real man is supposed to be more artistic than prescriptive? What if being a real man has to do more with incorporating a growing authenticity than it does with mastering a set of skills? What if the definition of manhood is far broader than you imagined? What if authenticity looked different for one man than it does for another?

It might seem a weird illustration, but let's think about masculinity in terms of art. No one would argue that van Gogh, Cezanne, Renoir, Picasso, and Michelangelo weren't artists. It would be hard to make a case for which artist is more important. And what if we then included great poets such as Homer, Dante, Chaucer, Shakespeare, Whitman, and Frost; and writers such as Steinbeck, Hemingway, Faulkner, Irving, and Mailer; and architects such as Wren, Saarinen, Pei, and Wright; and chefs such as Pépin, Keller, or Boulud? All these men expressed themselves differently with great impact and beauty.

Let's look at it another way—through the lens of sports. Can you compare Ty Cobb to Johnny Unitas or Wayne Gretzky? All great athletes, right? Each one of the best (if not *the* best) at what he did. But if Gretzky had tried to play baseball, he might have done okay, but he would not have been The Great One. Remember when Michael Jordan retired from basketball to play baseball and then golf?

Ralph Waldo Emerson said, "Every genuine work of art has as much reason for being as the earth and the sun." The Bible says the same thing a bit differently:

> When I look at the night sky and see the work
>   of your fingers—
>   the moon and the stars you set in place—
> what are mere mortals that you should think
>   about them,
>   human beings that you should care for
>   them?
> Yet you made them only a little lower than
>   God
>   and crowned them with glory and honor.[3]

What if this means each person is a unique work of art, as important as anyone else? What if the measure of a man is not what he does or what he accomplishes, but whether he is being himself as God reveals that to him? What if practicing authentic Christianity has less to do with our emulating Jesus and more to do with our increasingly becoming more of who we were made to be by God?

What if authentic manhood means living like Jesus and incorporating the principles he embodied in a way that helps us express our unique creative potential more fully (thus revealing the image of God more clearly)? What if we quit trying to be perfect, or be better, or be good, and instead spent our emotional and spiritual energy on trying to be ourselves?

What if spiritual maturity has more to do with our becoming more ourselves than it does with our making fewer mistakes? What if conforming to the image of Christ is more about living life in the same freedom and dependence that Jesus did, instead of losing our uniqueness to conform to a particular standard?

We think these are really important questions when considering what it means to be a *real man*.

If the goal of masculinity is an increasing authenticity through the work in our lives of love, faith, and hope, then the art of authentic manhood is something we will be practicing for the rest of our lives. In other words, maybe real manhood is a continual process of becoming, rather than something we attain, say, around the age of eighteen, twenty-one, or whatever age you want to suggest. Maybe that is what the Bible means when it talks about working out our salvation with fear and trembling.[4] We will never get this thing completely right, but that's by design. Becoming an artist is a life-long process, and we will be learning how to be "real men" for the rest of our days. What could be scarier—or more exciting—than that?

Art and Craft

There is a familiar parable about a man who lived near the site where a magnificent cathedral was being built. Fascinated by the work, the man faithfully spent time every day watching the work as the stone structure took shape. Over time, he caught the attention of the bishop who oversaw the construction, and the two men developed a friendship. The cathedral took many, many years to complete, and though the man was quite young when the cornerstone was laid, he had gray hair when the work was finally finished. As the work drew to an end, the bishop, who was quite old himself by then, asked the man to dinner so the two could quietly celebrate the cathedral's completion.

When they sat down to eat, the bishop thanked God for the food. As they ate, they reminisced about all the years that had passed and all that had transpired in the construction of the cathedral. "Friend, you have watched the work here daily for many years," the bishop said. "You know, perhaps more than I, the effort that went into the construction of this place. Tell me what you've seen."

There was a pause while the other man gathered his thoughts. He was a simple man who chose his words carefully. After considering the question for a long time, he said, "A laborer works with his hands. A craftsman works with his hands and his head. But an artist—he works with his hands, his head, and his heart."

To live as authentic men, we must be able to bring our entire selves to bear in our lives—our hands, our heads, and our hearts. There is a vast difference between painting by numbers and creating our own unique masterpieces.

Sadly, much of the Christian men's movement over the past two decades has taken the paint-by-numbers approach, encouraging men to work harder at being godly men, husbands, and fathers, and too often handing us tools, strategies, and techniques to "fix" our lives.

Case in point: I (Stephen) had lunch recently with a gentleman a few years older than I, who has served in significant leadership capacities in two very noteworthy parachurch ministries. During the course of our lunch, he asked me how I was doing. I told him about a remarkable men's group meeting I had attended that morning and how surprised I was by the way God chooses to work in people's lives. He then asked me how I was doing as a man. I told him I was lonely for my wife and kids and how my heart ached with a desire for more time with them. In response, the gentleman very humbly, respectfully, and kindly told me of some techniques he had instituted in his own family. "I date my kids regularly," he said. I politely nodded as he explained how he takes each of his kids out on dates, and how he never leaves the house to run an errand without one or two of his four kids in tow. He continued by telling me that when each of his children turned ten, he took them on a trip. "It has become a tradition in our family."

When he was done speaking, I politely thanked him for his suggestions, but inside I wanted to put my salad fork through his hand. I've been "dating" each of my kids regularly since they could walk. And once a year, my wife and I make a point of taking each of our four children away, just the three of us, for a long weekend. This guy was simply missing the point. I *spend* time with my family. I deeply love my family. He was honestly trying to help, but I wasn't looking for a solution as much as I was looking for compassion. I didn't want

HOW TO FIX THE TOILET

Picture this. You've just finished an enormous Mexican dinner, and you race home to relieve the pressure. You go to flush and—*wham-o*—the toilet overflows. (Remember *Along Came Polly*, with Ben Stiller?)

It's a tragedy, but it doesn't have to happen. Fellas, turn off the freakin' water when the business doesn't go down! The shut-off valve is usually at the base of the toilet where the water line comes out of the wall.

Before you try flushing again, grab the plunger and take care of the stoppage. If you don't own a plunger, go right now and get one. We're serious—go right now. There are no other suggestions that could be more valuable than this one.

Don't turn the water back on until the deuce is set free.

Most other toilet problems occur inside the tank, where the moving parts are located. Here are some simple ways to recognize and fix three common toilet problems. Before starting any repair, turn off the water-supply valve, as mentioned above. For simple repairs, you may or may not need to flush the water out of the tank.

Problem: Tank fills, but water still runs. Remove the tank cover and check the float arm. The float arm and ball may be connected by an L-shaped collar, which lets you raise or lower the float ball more easily. Only about half the float ball should be below water. If there's water inside the float ball, it won't rise high enough to close the valve. Unscrew the float ball and replace it with a new one.

Problem: Tank doesn't fill, and water still runs. A running toilet may be caused by a defect in the lift wire, the flush ball, or the flush valve. A worn flush ball may be the problem. If the rubber flush ball has hardened or is out of shape, purchase a replacement ball and screw it onto the end of the lift rod. You may wish to purchase a flapper-type replacement for the tank ball. A flapper unit has a longer lifespan and quieter flush than the conventional flush ball. Follow the manufacturer's installation instructions.

Problem: Toilet won't flush properly. If the toilet handle must be held down to complete the flushing action, first check the trip lever. The lever is set at a slight angle inside the tank so that it can operate without scraping the tank's side, the overflow tube, or the intake valve. If the trip lever isn't moving freely when you flip the handle, bend it slightly toward the center of the tank. As you bend it, use one hand to hold the lever in place where it joins the handle.

A second place to check is the lift wire. It may not be raising the flush ball high enough, and the outrushing water may be pulling it back down too quickly. Simply bend the lift wire enough to shorten it. The shorter lift wire will hold the flush ball out of the way of the rushing water until enough water has passed to clear the bowl.

An inadequate flush can also be caused by a float ball that is adjusted too low to allow a full tank of water. Bend the float arm upward to correct this. The water level in most tanks should be one-half to three-quarters of an inch below the top of the overflow pipe.

If all else fails or none of this makes any sense, call the plumber. There's a reason these guys charge so much money. They know things we don't. Don't deny a man his paycheck.

Adapted from www.fixatoilet.com and www.doityourself.com/stry/h2repairtoilet.

his help; I wanted his camaraderie. But instead I was handed *techniques*.

Painful Balancing Act

There is great pain in trying to be authentic men, balancing family, work, faith, hobbies, and other responsibilities in a way that reflects who we want to be. The pain of not being with the people we most love is inevitable.

From time to time, we all need some suggestions for how to live out our passions in this world, but too often we try to circumvent the pain of living in a broken world with strategies for success. But unless we as men have our hearts, all our strategies will be meaningless. By "have our hearts," we mean that we must be engaged in an ongoing and intimate relationship with ourselves. This has many facets—knowing how our past affects our present; being aware of our emotions; recognizing more and more the profound work of Christ's resurrection in our lives, and our response to it; and identifying how our unique styles of relating impede our relationships with God and others. But most of all, it speaks of the mysterious process by which, having recognized our powerlessness and yielded our hearts back over to God, we find—to our surprise—that we have more of what we gave away in the first place: We have our hearts.

The truth is, we can do "all the right things" perfectly, but if our hearts are not present, it will be nothing more than empty religion. This is what the book of Ecclesiastes is about—having it all, knowing it all, and doing it all right, but without our hearts engaged, which makes it all as empty as vapor.

Our willingness to live in the midst of heartache with a deep awareness of our feelings, needs, desires, longings, and hopes is essential for authentic manhood. When we live this way, we find that we get to the end of ourselves pretty quickly. Practicing the art of authentic manhood means that we acknowledge our willingness and desire to be transformed and our utter powerlessness to do anything worthwhile about it on our own. That is the beginning of being a "real man."

Lessons Learned

1. *Life is hard and painful.*
2. *Real men come in all shapes and sizes.*
3. *We'll never get manhood completely right.*
4. *It's not about techniques and trying harder.*
5. *Polyester ain't cotton.*

How to Move On from Here

To grow in the art of authentic masculinity, we must first expand our definition of being a "real man" beyond the stereotype of John Wayne and the "tips and techniques" approach of much of the recent men's movement. We need to better understand where our concepts of masculinity were formed.

A key component of practicing the art of authentic manhood is identifying the men (and women) who helped shape our ideas of masculinity (for better or worse). Likewise, we need to identify the ways in which we exercise our masculinity well and the ways in which we misuse our masculinity.

A third way to hone the art of real manhood is to find an environment that supports our maturity as men. For us, one of the most beneficial ways that we became deeply engaged in our own masculinity was through joining men's groups where the work of the group was focused on helping us live out our passions and develop an awareness of our feelings, needs, desires, longings, and hopes. These have been groups where other men worked to point things out that we couldn't see in ourselves—groups that invite authenticity (not just "accountability"). Some examples of these types of groups are the Samson Society, YMCA's Restore Ministries, or group counseling.

CHAPTER 2

Hide and Seek

The Art of Stepping Up

My (David's) basketball career began in the spring of 1979. I started out playing point guard for Burger Chef, one of the local fast-food joints that sponsored a team. We didn't have Burger King in my rural community, because sometimes the national chains just didn't stretch far enough to reach those little pockets of the South.

Now, when I say "rural," I mean *rural,* but not *rural* rural. For example, my grandparents' church didn't have running water until I was in middle school. (We just peed out in the woods.) But nobody handled snakes or married their cousins. (Well, maybe *some* people married their cousins, but most didn't.)

Every Saturday morning, my family piled into our big Oldsmobile and drove to the old elementary school gymnasium to watch me play my games. If the truth be told, they really came to watch me warm the bench for three quarters, and then if we were ahead by more than twenty points, I'd get to play a few minutes or so of the last quarter. I was the smallest boy on the team, and it would be safe to say I wasn't a strong contributor. My favorite part of the experience was the chocolate shakes and skinny fries at Burger Chef following the game. In case you're wondering, I didn't go on to play college ball or enter the NBA.

During the games, I sat on the bench beside my teammates, most of whom had banged down the door of puberty with force and fury. I, on the other hand, showed no indication of the onset of that particular rite of passage. I was small and scrawny, and my feet would swing back and forth without ever touching the gym floor. Most of my teammates were tall and gangly, with hairy legs and the beginning scents of adolescence. From my vantage point on the bench next to them, they smelled of repressed emotion, surges of testosterone, anger, and attitude. I still smelled of Legos, Hot Wheels, and innocence.

I still have our team photo from that year. We wore orange jerseys, white Lycra gym shorts, and tall white tube socks with orange stripes just below the knee (or in my case, closer to the thigh). Some of my teammates wore terry cloth brow bands that matched their white wristbands. I wore only the wristbands. I didn't need any additional accessories to add to the humiliation.

My shoulders weren't broad at all, and my frame was so small that my jersey often slid off one shoulder. As if it wasn't bad enough to be the smallest guy on the team, when my jersey slid to one side, I looked like the chick in *Flashdance*.

I had two coaches. I don't remember their names, for some reason, but the head coach looked like Grizzly Adams. He had a big, brown beard and always wore an orange nylon slick jacket with jeans. He never smiled. He just yelled a lot. His sidekick assistant coach was a short guy in his mid-fifties with greased-back hair, who always smelled of cigarette smoke and heavy aftershave. He looked like a character from *The Sopranos*. He yelled a lot too. He yelled at the referees, he yelled at us, and he yelled at his wife if she interrupted him for concessions money during the game.

I can't really remember what I did or what I thought about for the forty-five minutes to an hour that I sat and watched the Burger Chef boys run up and down the court. (I should have brought a good book, because I did a lot of sitting and waiting.) I do, however, remember my heart pounding when I was ordered over to the scorer's table to inform the guy holding the scorebook that the coach was putting me in.

There is one memory in particular that has profoundly shaped my response as a man in more ways than I care to consider. It was early in the season, and I was put into the game while my team had possession of the ball. I hustled over to the far side of the court and positioned myself to receive a pass. The ball went from the point guard to the center and back to the point guard. I remember that the other team seemed unusually fast and big that day. (Of course, they always seemed fast and big to me).

I was working as hard as I could to get open for a pass. The guy guarding me was working as hard as he could to make me unavailable. We continued this dance for a good thirty seconds—during which, at some point, it occurred to me that even if the ball should come to me, there was a great chance that this guy would easily (and successfully) block any attempt I'd make to pass or score. And my coach would start yelling and thinking to himself, *Why do I even bother putting that scrawny kid in the game?*

My solution to the problem? Look unavailable. I formulated a plan in my mind. *Don't make any great attempt to get open. Hide behind his blocking and only shift from time to time. It won't be that hard to position yourself to look unavailable. You're small, but he's bigger. You're fast, but he's much faster. And if you never handle the ball, you'll never risk humiliating yourself in front of Grizzly Adams and his sidekick, the Burger Chef boys,*

*your parents, and everyone else present for this ridiculous
spectacle.*

Let me tell you, it *worked*!

I began a dance of hiding that day that carried me
through the remainder of the season. Sometimes the
defensive players were slow, and sometimes they were
lazy (or maybe they, too, were thinking about chocolate shakes and skinny fries). Whatever the case, the
ball rarely came to me. When it did, I made a handful
of successful passes, but I rarely shot. And when I did
shoot, I usually missed. I made every attempt to avoid
getting fouled, because shooting free throws meant the
game stopped and all eyes were on you. In short, I mastered the art of hiding, and that strategy stayed with me
well into my adult life.

As I have aged, I have seen how the strategy of hiding has debilitated me at a number of points in my life.
I have hidden from opportunities; I have hidden from
friends; I have hidden from people at work; I have hidden from my wife—and even from my own children. I
have hidden with the belief that I have nothing of value
to contribute to the game. I think I lived twenty years of
my life like a benched player waiting on his number to
be called so he could step into the game—only to hide.

I have lived with the belief that my contribution will
be minimal at best, that the people around me would

HOW TO SINK A FREE THROW

Anyone can learn to sink a free throw, but if you've watched any of the NBA, you know that not everyone is willing to learn and practice the proper technique. Rick Barry was one of the best free-throw shooters in NBA history. He shot the ball granny style, like Ollie in *Hoosiers,* and hit almost 95 percent of his free throws during his career. How sweet is that? The key is to find a form you are comfortable with and repeat that form over and over. The more repetition, the easier it becomes. Here are the basics:

1. Stand at the free-throw line with your feet shoulder-width apart and parallel to one another, both feet pointing toward the basket.

2. Lightly cradle and support the ball with your non-shooting hand. Place the fingertips of your shooting hand on the seams of the ball, with your thumb and palm acting as supports.

3. Keeping your shooting forearm straight (avoid tilting it side to side), raise the ball slightly above your chest.

4. Aim for a target just above the rim, and try not to shoot the ball short. A good target is the back of the rim (where it meets the backboard).

5. Bend your knees. An accurate shot doesn't rely on arm strength; it uses leg strength to propel the ball upward.

6. In one fluid motion, shoot the ball, uncoiling from your knees through your arm, releasing the ball with your fingertips. You want to create a soft arc with the shot and put backspin on it by using your fingertips. Follow through by bending your shooting hand forward, as if you're reaching for the rim (like reaching into a cookie jar).

The truth about free throws is that they're all about repetition and concentration. Think about it. You're only fifteen feet away from a rim that's only ten feet off the ground. The circumference of the rim is double the size of the basketball. How hard can it really be? Not hard at all—unless you're Shaquille O'Neal. But we'll extend the guy some grace. (If you wanna know what it's like for Shaq, try shooting a tennis ball. That's how big the guy's hands are.)

be better served if I never got my hands on the ball. And the enemy has been victorious. I have been silent when I should have spoken. I have stood back when I should have stepped forward. I have lived in fear and shame. There was little to no chance that I could live out of any place of who I was designed to be.

Perhaps the most defining moment of this came in my mid-twenties. I met my wife as an undergraduate at the University of Tennessee. She was a graduate student at the time. Connie was one of the most fascinating, intelligent, compassionate, beautiful women I had ever encountered. The more time we spent together, the more infatuated I became with her.

She finished her graduate work and took a job outside the city, deep in the Great Smoky Mountains, working at a home and school for boys who had been abandoned by life in some capacity. I can remember visiting her at the Ranch the first time and watching her interact with these broken children who had been dealt a lousy hand when God shuffled the family-of-origin cards. I was so overwhelmed by her—her passion, her tenderness, her compassion, her beauty, her commitment, her courage, her joy. I watched her, and I knew that I wanted to spend the rest of my life with this woman.

I actually felt *ready* to be called into the game. But

my pattern had always been to enter the game and immediately become unavailable. And as desperately as I wanted to marry her, I just couldn't do it. I couldn't propose. So I just continued to date her. *Dating is a good thing. I'm not jumping ship on the relationship; I'm just staying put.* But the truth is, I was hiding. I hid in this long-term dating relationship. I was both available and unavailable. Weeks turned into months. Months turned into a year, and I managed to somehow avoid ever handling the ball. She would subtly bring up conversations about commitment and marriage, and I would dodge the ball.

As I stalled and stalled and stalled, Connie grew weary. Weary and sad. Her passion and her joy began to subside. Her longing turned to hopelessness. Our relationship, once marked by romance and happiness, became defined by tension and conflict, loneliness and disconnect.

One morning, a year into my stalling and hiding, I had breakfast with Carter, my good friend and pastor. It was one of the dozens of times in my life as a man, a husband, and a father that Carter and I have had an extremely disruptive conversation. We made small talk for the first fifteen minutes, and then he looked at me across the table and asked (very gently at first) how my relationship with Connie was going. I gave him some kind of vague response that he bypassed quickly, and then he shot me this question: "Why are you so afraid of getting married?"

I nearly spewed my coffee all over his shirt. "What did you say?"

"You heard what I said."

He just sat and stared at me for what felt like hours. And then, with the deepest sense of compassion and strength, he said, "What scares you so much?"

I couldn't answer him. I couldn't really speak at all. I just sat frozen, my heart pounding, and then I grabbed for a pen on the table and began scribbling all over the napkin in front of me:

> I'm afraid to be a husband.
> I'm afraid I'll screw it all up.
> I'm afraid I have absolutely nothing of value to offer anyone.
> I'm afraid of having kids.
> I'm afraid I'm not capable of leading a family.
> I'm afraid I don't have the right ingredients to be a real man.
> I'm afraid of being a grown-up.
> I'm afraid of showing up.

I kept writing and writing and writing. I covered both sides of the napkin. He just let me write for a while and kept reading my words from across the table. He waited, and then he said, "Yeah, me too."

I paused for a moment, and then I pushed back: "How can you be scared of being a husband or a father? You're already doing both! You're already a grown-up!"

He laughed and said, "In theory, I am a grown-up. I'm obviously a husband and a father, but it doesn't mean I'm not terrified and confused about what I'm doing, David."

I remember feeling such freedom in his words, and how rare it was to be given permission by another man to just be *scared to death*.

We talked about men and fear for some time. We talked about how debilitating fear can be, how afraid we are as men of the power we don't have and the power that we do. Fear was paralyzing me. Carter knew this, and somewhere in there, so did I.

He went on to say, "David, it's fine for you to feel scared, but you need to deal with your fear and quit stalling."

I went from feeling relief to feeling some fear again about where he might be going with his next words. He continued, "I'm gonna shoot straight with you. Connie is an incredible woman. You know that, and so do I. She deserves more than a man who is planning to just date her for the next five years." I could agree with everything so far. It was his next sentence that sent me into orbit.

He leaned in toward me, shifted in his chair, and began speaking with greater authority. His words even sounded sharper. "I think it would be a good idea for her to date other people."

He could have shot me in between the eyes with a BB gun, and I would have been less surprised.

"What did you say?"

Again he answered, "You heard what I said."

He was, in essence, saying to me, "Handle the ball, or get out of the game!" He was challenging me to quit hiding.

There was something that shifted in me in that moment. I went from being terrified to being angry. I was angry at Carter for what he said, but even more angry at the truth of his words.

It turned out to be the kind of anger that emerges in a man when he is full of passion and someone challenges him to live authentically out of who he was designed to be. It was magical. I thought to myself, *Like hell she is dating other people. Over my dead body.* I don't recall, but I'm certain that Carter was smiling the entire time as he witnessed this shift beginning in me.

We finished our time, and I called a therapist on the way home and booked myself an appointment. I began exploring my story. I went chasing after a ten-year-old boy who had played benchwarmer guard for Burger Chef, the one who had started hiding and dodging and stalling.

The shift in me that morning was the beginning of a powerful evolution that would continue over the course of the next year and into the next decade.

And I got married less than a year from that day.

Stepping onto the Court

Until that day when Carter confronted me, I was a man disconnected from my own story and my own heart. I was a man who wouldn't ask questions and didn't want to remember. This inability or unwillingness to engage with the world around me opened the door to so many destructive possibilities. Stepping onto the court and coming out of hiding involved asking questions. And these questions inevitably led to something valuable. Asking questions required exploration, which ultimately led to a deeper connection—with my heart, with other people, and with God. Getting there, of course, required a great deal of remembering, some of which was deeply painful. I had to come to grips with the memory of being the smallest guy on the team—and all the hiding and fear and shame that

HOW TO TAKE A PUNCH

"I'm a lover, not a fighter."

That's all fine and dandy, but if some joker's hittin' on your lady or bad talkin' your mama, you need to be ready to throw down. And the key to success at fisticuffs is the ability to take a punch as well as dish one out.

Taking a punch is like eating broccoli . . . the more you do it, the more your body becomes accustomed. Allowing a friend to punch you in the face and stomach is a good place to start. When you get to the place where you don't flinch anymore, you know you're ready. Bullies expect you to flee in fear. Facing up to them is half of the battle. For the other half, let's look at some practical steps.

First and foremost, steer clear of getting hit. If possible, outmaneuver your foe. Stay outside his range. Usually you'll see it coming—you *know* when somebody throws a punch. When you *feel* the punch coming, take a diagonal step forward. If you time it right, the other guy will punch thin air, and you'll now be standing next to him, close enough to deliver a counter-punch. What you want to do now is "stun and run." Here are your options:

1. **FIST IN THE LOWER BACK (OTHERWISE KNOWN AS A KIDNEY PUNCH).** Hit him on the side of his spine, as low as possible.

2. **FIST TO THE BASE OF THE NECK.** Strike the bend where the shoulder becomes the neck.

3. **FIST OR ELBOW TO THE SCHNOZ.** Hit him as hard as you can in the nose, preferably with the base of the palm.

4. **FIST TO THE RIB CAGE, OR SLIGHTLY BELOW.** He'll be thinking about taking his next breath while you skedaddle.

5. **KNEE TO THE NUTS.** (No explanation needed.)

Remember, the Bible teaches that it's better to give rather than to receive. Now, *run*! Get the heck out of there, and live to see another day.

If getting hit is inevitable, keep the following principles in mind:

1. **AVOID A DIRECT BLOW.** Deflect or block blows with your fists and forearms. Protect your ribs and chest with your upper arms.

2. **GO INSIDE.** (Move your feet. Don't just lean.) Get in close to the attacker. If you're in close, he can't extend on his punches. However, watch out for knees, head butts, and elbows. Those are *very* effective at close quarters.

3. **DON'T PANIC!** If you panic, you will have a hard time recovering from a hard blow. You'll be surprised how fast your body will recover after a solid punch. As you near middle age, your recovery time will increase, but you'll be losing your memory by then anyway, so don't sweat it.

accompanied my role as a benchwarmer who wanted to play and yet didn't want to get into the game.

As men, we are called by God to remember:

> Only be careful, and watch yourselves
> closely so that you do not forget the
> things your eyes have seen or let them
> slip from your heart as long as you
> live. Teach them to your children and
> to their children after them."[1]

And guys, note that there is no disclaimer; there's nothing that says, "You can forget the things your eyes have seen if they've been painful." There's no separate category for "letting things slip from your heart" if they involved being wounded or harmed. We are called to remember the *entire* story. The good and the bad. The joy and the sorrow. The clean and the messy.

Frederick Buechner speaks to the *redemptive value* of remembering the entire story, in his memoir *Telling Secrets:*

> Memory makes it possible for us both
> to bless the past, even those parts of
> it that we have always felt cursed by,
> and also to be blessed by it. If this

kind of remembering sounds like
what psychotherapy is all about, it is
because of course it is, but I think it is
also what the forgiveness of sins is all
about—the interplay of God's forgiveness of us and our forgiveness of God
and each other.[2]

Remembering is a foundational ingredient in regaining, restoring, and redeeming our lives as men created in the image of God. It is through remembering that we are able to reclaim the parts of our lives that we had long since forgotten or buried.

Remembering our stories (both good and bad, painful and joyful) reminds us of the power of a second chance and reconnects us to God, who joins us in the broken and forgotten places. Not only does God join us in those places we've stashed away as too painful to revisit, but he also transforms those memories into something of value and purpose. The crap of our lives, when we surrender it to the hands of God, becomes the fertilizer of our future.

Shooting Hoops

I saw God's redemptive power played out in my relationship with my sons when they were very young. Despite not having *any* genetic gifting, my boys seem to *love* the game of basketball. When they were eighteen months old and we would walk down the hall of the YMCA where I do my workouts, they would peer through the glass at the court, point, and go nuts. When there was a game going on, they would paste themselves to the glass and watch in fascination. So we began a ritual of shooting some hoops after I finished my workout. The twins would scream every time I stripped the net. Then they'd chase down the ball and beg me to do it again. After a while, they demanded to be put on my shoulders and taken close to the goal so they could attempt a few shots themselves.

One morning, we were in the midst of our basketball ritual when it struck me that at some point, in the not-so-faraway future, my boys would discover that their dad's basketball career (and skill, for that matter) peaked and ended as a ten-year-old backup point guard for Burger Chef. They'd find out that the Magic Johnson they thought I was when they were eighteen months old wasn't quite so magical on the court. I realized, standing mid-court with a boy on my shoulders holding a basketball, that the realities of my incompetence would be exposed in a matter of years.

Well, we're there now. We put a basketball goal in our backyard a couple of years ago, so now we play together at home. I'm still lousy; they're improving. And I'm free enough to just shoot hoops with my boys, not buried in shame and contempt, and enjoy being in their presence. Who cares that I stink at the game? Those two guys are only interested in my showing up and stepping onto the court. They just want a man who enjoys some of the things they love and is interested in being in their company. They'll likely continue to improve their game over time. And who knows, maybe I will too. If not, we'll just hang out at Burger Chef and have chocolate shakes and skinny fries once it's all said and done.

Clumsy Does As Clumsy Can

We know this is totally obvious, but it has to be said: Central to our authenticity as men is the concept of being genuine. And the key to authenticity is discovering our uniqueness. Sure, we all have a lot in common as men, but it's our individuality that enables us to live authentic lives. We were not created as fakes, replicas, imitations, or phonies. We're each an original, one of a kind. But when we try to practice our masculinity as a reproduction of someone else's uniqueness, we come across as, at best, insincere.

Here's the thing: When we seek to live in an authentic way, we will make a bunch of mistakes. We will screw it up big time. But the litmus test of an authentic man is his willingness to make a fool of himself for what matters most to him. Being authentic means showing up and stepping onto the court of life, regardless of our perceived skills. It's being willing to shoot baskets with your kids even when you play like Pee Wee Herman.

A friend of ours, Dr. Chip Dodd, is the founder of an addiction treatment center for impaired professionals, called the Center for Professional Excellence, in Nashville. For more than a decade, doctors, lawyers, pastors, pharmacists, dentists, and executives have come from all over the country for help in dealing with the causes and complications of drug, alcohol, or sex addiction (and sometimes all three at once), as well as severe depression and anxiety. At some point in the treatment process, Chip inevitably asks each man, "What would you give for your father to have been clumsy?" He invites his patients to consider what their childhood would have been like if they'd had the kind of dad that messed up, got scared openly, gave himself fully to the process of living, made mistakes, was prepared to not know, was willing to make an idiot of himself, and cleaned up his messes as best he could. To a man, every patient for ten years has said (often through tears) something to the effect of, "Every dime I've ever made." When we live our lives protected and guarded, those around us end up paying the price.

Guarded Hearts Gone Wrong

My (Stephen's) son Elijah got a copy of *Toy Story* for his third birthday. For months after watching the movie, he ran around the house, jumping off furniture and shouting, "To infinity and beyond!" At three, he could easily tap into the authentic desires of his heart to fight for truth and honor. It saddens me that, as he gets older, his dreams will fade and he, too, will become *practical*.

Did you have big dreams, too, when you were young? Did you hope to one day become a fireman, a superhero, a race car driver, or an astronaut? Ah, but somewhere along the way, your wishes became more reasonable. Your hopes became fantasies, childhood daydreams that were easy to discount. You settled for more responsible goals: accountant, businessman, pastor, salesman, teacher, chemist . . . you get the idea. Somehow, you learned not to dream quite so big. You figured you'd better keep your expectations small and manageable and reasonable.

The problem is that living authentically as God's image bearers is neither practical nor predictable. We were made by God to desire deeply. We're hungry for the experience of being fully alive. God designed us

HOW TO DO A SWAN DIVE

It's always a treat to see someone else do a belly flop—otherwise known as the "smack and sink." You don't wanna be that guy, so here are a few tips that will give your dive an Olympic-style presentation.

1. The launch is essential to a successful swan dive. The best swan dives are done from springboards. Take a few steps, and as you approach the end of the board, lift one knee up and push off the other leg, landing on two feet at the end of the board. (When you land, your body should be perfectly vertical.) Keep your head up as you jump—if not, you'll tumble forward and hit the water with your back. (Ouch!) As you bounce off the board, keep your head upward, and raise your arms over your head.

2. Wait until you're at the top of the dive, then reach down and touch your toes. (This is called a *jackknife.*)

3. Right before you hit the point of no return, bring your hands together, put your head down, and bend your torso toward the water. (If you flub this step, get ready for the smack and sink, 'cause you're belly flopping, baby.)

4. Now, lift your legs, point your toes, and try to get your body as straight as possible before hitting the water. Clasp your hands together in a fist, and punch a hole through the water to create minimal splash.

5. Unless you're built like Michael Phelps (which, more than likely, you're not), do not wear a Speedo. In fact, there is never an occasion for a guy over the age of sixteen who is not competing on a swim team to wear a Speedo. We repeat: *never.*

for pleasure, delight, and joy. We ache to the core for moments of complete freedom and acceptance.

Here's the rub: We know for sure that life will kick us in the teeth. We've learned that living fully is risky, so we've backed off. We've dialed it down. After all, it's not practical to want to grow up to be Spiderman. It's not possible to major in superhero at college. Yet, no matter how hard we try, as adult men, we cannot stop hoping. We can't short-circuit our hearts.

But how do we cope in a world where struggle, disappointment, and failure are inevitable? How do we deal with the fact that our dads dropped the ball and we've dropped it ourselves with our own kids? Surely there must be a way to overcome our weaknesses. That's why the lure of being perfect is so powerful. We all want to be in control.

MINE! MINE! MINE!

The lure of control is a perceived shortcut that promises to satisfy a godly desire, longing, or hope for something better, while at the same time mitigating the risk of disappointment, abandonment, betrayal, or failure. In other words, we want to have all that life has to offer, without risking pain, heartache, or difficult choices. We want to be in the driver's seat. We want to have our cake and eat it too, and for it not to have any calories.

A man's specific lures to control are primarily based on his relational woundedness. In that way, temptation to be in power is directly tied to a man's individual story. (Like David and his basketball dreams.) The temptation to be in control is rooted in meeting a legitimate need in an illegitimate way. When we act on these temptations, they become what the Bible calls sin.

A great definition of sin is "taking control over what is God's." Sin is always an effort to satisfy a true desire of the heart on our own terms, without needing to depend on God. The human heart will do whatever it takes to have its needs met—legitimately or otherwise.

When we *attempt* to seek relief using illegitimate means, we set ourselves up for some really hard lumps. We try using counterfeit fulfillments to control life so that we don't have to feel pain or trust God. It's always an attempt to escape from life's shame, sadness, and loneliness. We've been conditioned through pain to try to manage life.

Selfishness and self-protection are much more attitudes of the heart than they are behaviors. They reveal a lack of trust in God. We must understand how our stories have shaped us if we want to live authentically, because we must regularly practice recognizing the parts of our stories in which we doubt God's goodness and fail to see his delight in us.

Thinking about God in the right way will never alleviate our need to disclose the truth of our hearts to him. Contending with God in the hard parts of our lives and experiencing his goodness, love, power, and perfection will transform us in ways we've never expected or even dared dream.

Struggling with God is not a sin. It's not wrong. It's a place that God lets us come to in order to reveal, clarify, and set apart our hearts. Self-reliance is never okay. It turns into spiritual arrogance, which is depending too heavily on our own understanding of God as a substitute for faith. It is faithlessness that says, "If I think about God correctly, life will be okay."

Painting with Color

How then does a guy figure out how to become authentic? Well, for starters, you could go to seminary. Isn't that where guys go to really know about God? Okay, maybe not seminary, but how about church? Well, no. Who do you know at church who is really authentic? Church is full of hypocrites and sinners, right? You could study the Bible more; it has all the answers to life. Yeah, right. We've been studying Scripture for several thousand years and only one guy ever really understood it—Jesus—and he was God.

It's not that seminary, church, and Bible study are bad. It's that they aren't worth much unless we are willing to personally struggle with God. For us to live authentically as men, we must come face-to-face with the parts of our stories where it seems to us that God has let us down. And then we must contend with him in those places. The proving ground for authentic manhood is always getting into the ring with God.

Have you ever wondered why God lets us go through things that hurt so much? Why a God who says he loves us doesn't keep us from moments of shame and heartache?

I (Stephen) really began to wrestle with this in a new way a few years ago, when one of my closest friends died in a snowmobile accident. Kevin was my longest-standing friend, and his death hit me hard. I remember hearing the news after coaching a soccer game in Alabama. I fell to the ground in the middle of the field and cried out in anger and grief. I lay in the field, weeping, in front of several hundred people.

At Kevin's wake, person after person got up and told story after story of how he had affected their lives with his kindness, humor, quest for adventure, and passion for the outdoors. His death made me stop and ask myself some really hard questions, look at my life and examine who I was, where I've been, and where I was heading. I had to decide for myself: Was I going to follow everybody else's rules for how to be me, or was I going to risk being myself? Death strips away everything that life in this world has given us—everything but our stories. I had to decide what kind of story I wanted my life to tell. Would it be clean and sterile and safe? Or would it be messy and real and full?

When you think of your own story, who is writing the script? What standards are you trying to live up to? How high is the bar you are trying to jump? Do you have freedom to drop the ball? What are the scenes in your life that make you laugh, and which ones make you cry?

What part of your story reflects the bigger story of Christ—a story of hope, love, and liberation? And what part of your story is unresolved, and exposes your disbelief in the gospel, and brings you shame?

Which scenes cause you to doubt God's love and your hope that everything will be set right? Where have you hidden? Where have you allowed shame and failure to define you?

Wherever we are bound by shame, anxiety, or depression, we live outside the power of the gospel. If the first step toward authenticity is admitting that life is really painful, then the second step is showing up to face the pain. Learning to live honestly with our hearts in times of failure and pain is essential to learning the art of showing up.

We are pretty big deals. Not because of what we do or how we think, but rather for who made us and whose image we reflect. Maybe it's not our job to succeed at anything; instead, maybe it's our privilege to walk into the valley of our own messed-up stories with the hope of encountering a God who will set things straight. Maybe that is what it looks like to practice the art of showing up.

Lessons Learned

1. *Every man will be scared spitless.*
2. *Remembering your story is redemptive.*
3. *Stepping onto the court and getting in the game make a real difference.*
4. *Be clumsy.*
5. *Don't play with snakes, and never marry a cousin.*

How to Move On from Here

"Showing up" as men requires that we remember the past and reclaim the parts of our stories that we have tried to bury or forget. Make a list of the important scenes from your life. Pick one or two of the most significant and share them with another person who is important to you. If you need help getting started with this, a great place to begin is with Dan Allender's book *To Be Told: Know Your Story, Shape Your Future.* There's even a workbook to go along with it.

As you begin to explore your story, an important step is to identify where some common themes of shame emerge. Often from these moments, we create tendencies that recur over and over again. To be more fully present as a man, you need to recognize how your shame thwarts your relationships and your dreams.

Showing up requires that we quit faking it. Practice saying "I don't know" when you don't know. I (Stephen) am so bad at this that one of my friends nicknamed me "Holiday" after the guys on the Holiday Inn Express commercials who pretend to be experts. Don't act like those guys. True genuineness comes from a willingness to be clumsy. At all costs, be yourself.

CHAPTER 3

Soft Curves and Softer Lips

The Art of the Fairer Sex

You'd be hard pressed to find a grown man who would identify middle school as one of the most enjoyable times in his life. It's that period in a boy's development that is plagued with intense change—physically, emotionally, and relationally. Many developmental theorists describe this season as one of the worst episodes in a boy's life. It was hands down one of the worst times of my (David's) life. When I look at my school pictures from seventh and eighth grade, my back gets tense, I start gritting my teeth, and an ache develops deep in my gut.

I have a photograph from a seventh-grade Sadie Hawkins dance that is particularly painful. I was asked by Shannon, one of the tallest girls in my grade. She was a really nice girl and it was a really nice gesture, but I was the shortest guy in my grade, so it was a really *bad* idea. But I went anyway, thankful to have been asked.

I don't know what dances were like at your school, but at mine no one really ever danced, except for the slow songs. The guys stood on one side of the gymnasium, and the girls congregated on the other side. (Unless they were going back and forth in groups to the bathroom, to giggle and look at themselves.) The faculty served punch and concessions. The P.E. teacher, Coach Looper, wandered around with the math and science teachers, looking for anyone who was trying to sneak under the bleachers to kiss or smoke.

There was always a theme, which was reflected in the photo backdrop and props at the dance. My seventh-grade year, the Sadie Hawkins dance took place mid-fall, around Halloween, and had a harvest theme. If it had been a Halloween dance, Shannon and I could've gone as Nicole Kidman and Tom Cruise (or Tom Cruise and anybody else). At the very least, we could've made something creative out of being so painfully mismatched.

Instead, we were stuck posing on hay bales with giant cornstalks and scarecrows behind us. The standard pose involved the girl sitting on a bale of hay and the guy standing behind her with one foot on the hay bale and kneeling forward with one elbow propped on his knee. Even though Shannon was seated, she was still taller than I was. When the photographer framed us in the camera, he realized the awkwardness of the moment. So he gently said, "Fella, why don't you just stand up for the shot." I took my foot off the hay bale and stood with my hands in my pockets. Even though Shannon was still seated and I was now fully standing, she was *still* taller. It was getting worse by the minute. "Just please take the picture," I begged, wanting to avoid drawing any more attention than necessary.

Well, I survived that experience, and three months passed before it was time to start thinking about the Valentine's dance. It was my turn to do the asking. There weren't many girls who were shorter than I was, so I had my eyes set on a particular girl in my grade, who was still taller than I was, but only a head taller. If she'd been seated on a hay bale, I would have towered over her. (Well, I would have at least held my own.) She was beautiful. She had deep brown eyes and long, flowing hair that parted in the middle and feathered back on both sides, like Farrah Fawcett in *Charlie's Angels*. For purposes of this story, I'm just going to call her "Farrah."

Not only was Farrah beautiful, she also had breasts. Real breasts, unlike most of her thirteen-year-old counterparts. And breasts are just fascinating to a seventh-grade boy. (Remember the Christmas pageant scene in *Simon Birch*?) Farrah was in my band class. She played the clarinet and I played the trumpet. The brass section was seated two rows behind the wind section in a semicircle. We were on opposite sides of the room, which meant I could stare across the room at her beautiful, round . . . eyes. She was so out of my league, but I thought if I asked her far enough in advance, no one else would have gotten to her yet. And some girls like small guys. They find them rather cute, like a little chimp or a puppy. I was hoping she liked puppies a lot.

So, one day, after packing up my trumpet and heading for the door, I found myself directly behind her. I followed her out of the band room, into the hallway, and then I walked up beside her. "Hi," I said, trying to look like a cute little Labrador retriever.

She smiled and looked down at me, like she might want to pet me. I decided to just go for it.

"I was wondering if you wanted to go to the Valentine's dance with me. I mean, if you were planning to *go to* the Valentine's dance. And if you weren't planning to go *with* anyone else, that is. I mean, I'd like to take you if you were planning to *go* and not with someone else, then I'd like you to go with me."

Thankfully, she put us both out of our misery and stopped me from saying more (or the same thing over and over again). "Sure, I'll go."

I smiled and thought to myself, *She does like puppies.*

"Great. That's great. That's great that you were planning to go. That you wanted to go and no one else has asked you to go. I mean, I'm sure somebody was *about* to ask you. Probably *a lot* of people were about to ask you. But no one had asked you *yet*. And I did. And now we're going together. That's great."

She smiled again and said, "Yeah, that's great." And then she headed toward her locker, looked back and flipped her long, flowing hair, and said, "See you later, little one."

Okay, that's not what she said, but I was so happy at that moment that I honestly wouldn't have cared if she did. I waved good-bye to Farrah and headed to my next class, where I spent the entire hour thinking about her.

Weeks passed. I bought myself a new pair of parachute pants and one of those cool shirts that had a half collar (like a priest) that were in style back in the mid-eighties. Farrah and I made plans to meet at the dance, and we found each other in the lobby. She wanted to take a picture early so her freshly feathered hair would look its best, so we stood in the dreaded photo line. This time, it was a hot-air-balloon theme. They had a mock basket that couples stood inside, with streamers climbing upward to a large, heart-shape hot-air balloon. There was no kneeling or sitting in this photo, which meant we simply stood side by side, accentuating the height difference. On any other night, I would have slipped right into all the shame and humiliation that I normally experienced by being a short guy. Tonight, however, I found myself full of anticipation. For weeks, I had been looking forward to the chance to slow dance with her. *God is redeeming my sadness,* I thought to myself.

We finished our photo session and headed back to the gym. They were finishing a Phil Collins set. "Sussudio" was ending, and the mood changed as Phil crooned:

> Please give me one more night.
> Give me just one more night.

Yes, Phil, yes, I thought to myself. It was the perfect moment, the perfect music. Farrah and I swayed slowly, pressed tightly against each other, and turned in circles. I nestled my head under her chin. *Ecstasy!*

The night continued . . . Soft Cell sang "Tainted Love," Spandau Ballet sang "True," Pat Benatar sang "Shadows of the Night," and then my perfect evening came to a perfect close. Farrah's mom was waiting in the pick-up line outside the gym. A few cars behind, I could see my dad. We shared an awkward good-bye, and I told her I'd see her on Monday in band class.

HOW TO LOVE A WOMAN

Are we seriously writing a sidebar on this topic?

The truth is that loving a woman is one of the easiest and hardest things in the world to do. We love them because they're different. And we struggle to love them because they're *so* different. But we do love them, don't we? We often just don't know how to show it.

Because this is just a brief sidebar, our focus here will be on a woman's emotional need to know and be known. Men typically aren't very good at talking about how they're feeling. Nor are we good at listening to how a woman is really feeling. We'd rather fix things, right? We work hard to fix ourselves when something is wrong, and we work hard to fix our female counterparts when something is wrong with them.

But if you want to love a woman in a way that will be meaningful to her, learn to just *be* with her in her emotions. Probe how she's *feeling*; don't focus on how to fix it. Allow her to cry on your shoulder without trying to *solve* the problem.

Just as important, invite her into your inner life. Let her see your heart. What are you passionate about? What makes you sad? What are your hopes, desires, and dreams? What hurts you? Let's put aside the notion that loving a woman well means being a stud in the bedroom. That's your idea of being a "man," not hers. Her need is to have her emotional tank filled. And when it's filled, you'll know it. (We're speaking to husbands here. You single guys go take a cold shower and file this for later.)

I thought about her the entire rest of the weekend. I could hardly wait to see her again. That weekend would be the only time in my life that I actually looked forward to playing the trumpet.

On Monday, I walked into class and took my seat. Farrah was nowhere to be found. The bell was about to ring. I went from glaring at the clock to glaring at her empty seat in the wind section. Within eight seconds of the bell ringing, she pushed open the door and came running in. I watched her race to her seat, although in my mind it played out in slow motion, with Phil Collins providing the soundtrack. I watched her unpack and assemble her clarinet, apply the reed, and lick it as clarinet players do (I think to avoid that squeaking sound). Phil Collins continued to sing in my head, and I thought, *One more night, give me just one more night. . . .*

After class, Farrah approached me and said, "I had a really great time at the dance. We should do it again sometime." This time, I couldn't speak at all in her presence. I just panted like a happy puppy. She went on to say, "Anyhow, my parents are sponsors for the high school band, because my brother is a drummer, and the band is competing at some college in a couple of weekends, and I wondered if you wanted to go. The competitions are kind of boring, having to sit and listen to all these bands perform. But I thought, since I've got to go, maybe we could hang out. Want to?"

I couldn't believe what I had just heard. I nodded my head and continued panting. I think I might have said, "Yeah . . . sure."

"Great," she said. "Ask your parents and let me know."

Everything worked out as planned, and I got to take the hour-and-a-half drive with her and her parents. They didn't seem to mind having me along for the ride. In fact, they seemed to also see me as a harmless little puppy, like their daughter's new pet.

I don't remember anything about the band competition that day, though it was an all-day affair; I only remember the trip home. By the time we stopped for dinner at Shoney's and then loaded up for the final leg of the drive, it was after ten o'clock at night. That meant we wouldn't get home until almost midnight.

Her parents drove this big old van. Not like a minivan, but like a party van. It was huge, with multiple rows of leather captain's chairs, and the interior was kind of disco and tripped out. This was also back in the days when nobody wore seat belts. So her mom threw some blankets down in the back and said we could go to sleep on the ride home if we wanted.

Okay, let me detour here for a moment. I don't know

what in the heck this woman was thinking, but don't let your thirteen-year-old kid get horizontal in any location, for any reason, with someone of the opposite sex. Not in the back of a van, not in the middle of a field, not on a trampoline, not in the den watching a movie, not even floating on their backs in the middle of a swimming pool. Just don't do it. It's a bad idea.

Needless to say, *I* was thrilled by the idea of lying down anywhere with Farrah. We began just talking. Talking about the dance. Talking about people in band class. Talking about school. And then we started kissing. Kissing and kissing and kissing. And then all of a sudden she put her tongue in my mouth. It turned to wet, sloppy kissing that seemed strange and fascinating all at once. My eyes flew open. (Thankfully, I found her eyes were closed, so she couldn't see the panic and confusion in mine.) I was certain I had heard that this was how people got mono. I was sure I would have it by Monday, and my mom would know that I had been French kissing.

But it went even further than that. Farrah had been playing with my hair, but now she grabbed my hand and put it on top of her sweater. If she could have seen my eyes at that moment, she would have stopped kissing me and started administering CPR. Right then, her mother yelled back, "We're gonna stop and get gas if either of you needs to go to the bathroom."

I yanked my hand off Farrah's chest, reclaimed my tongue, and yelled, "I will! I need to go to the bathroom!"

I popped my head up over the seat. My hair was wildly tousled, and I was obviously still wearing panic on my face, because when I returned from the pit stop, Farrah's mother invited the two of us to sit on the row behind them. I couldn't sleep. You would've thought I'd had a Red Bull at the gas station, because I was wide awake for the remainder of the ride. Fully awake.

Thankfully, I didn't have mono when I awoke the next morning. And when my parents asked me how the trip had been, I said, "Fine," and gave them no other information, like a good, little seventh-grade boy. But Farrah must have read my fear and lack of experience, because on Monday she seemed less interested in me than ever.

Looking back on that night, I don't remember how long I functioned with the belief that you get mono from French kissing or that you grow hair on your palms if you masturbate. As a therapist working with fathers and sons, I am constantly amazed and terrified at how little information boys have about their own sexual development and about relationships with females. Young men don't have the correct information—heck, most of them don't have *any* information.

Engaging the opposite sex and understanding their own masculinity is just one big game of trial and error they have to face as they move from boyhood to manhood.

Set Sail, Gilligan

One thing's for sure: How we relate with the opposite sex says more about who we are as guys than who they are as women.

Men and women have been struggling in their relationships for a long, long, long time (like, since Adam and Eve). Though a relationship with a woman can be one of the most life-giving experiences a man can have, it can also be akin to walking barefoot across a bed of hot coals. You've heard that it can be done, and you may have even seen someone do it, but that gives you little insight or comfort that you yourself will make it across un-charred.

How is a guy to succeed when so many before him have failed? There is a mysterious art to engaging the fairer sex, and if a guy wants to achieve the kind of relationship with a woman that can change his life, he has to realize a few things first.

A relationship with a woman is more like sailing a boat than driving a car. In a car, you just fill 'er up with gas, fasten the seatbelt, put the pedal to the metal, and make sure you don't wreck. But in sailing, there's so much more to understand. You have to know how to read the wind (where it's coming from, how unpredictable it is, and the invisible power within it); you need to understand your equipment (jib, boom, rudder, spinnaker, etc.); and you have to accept that you only get better with experience. If you don't have a growing knowledge about such things, you will just sit there . . . or, worse, capsize . . . or, even worse, drown.

Where a lot of guys get it wrong with women is in not understanding God's hope for relationships between the sexes. Relationship is the most important thing to God. (No, not just *one* of the most important things—*the* most important thing.) We were created *by* love and *through* love *to be* loved and *to give* love.

Love changes things. When love is added to a relationship, it creates a reaction that provides the emotional and spiritual energy for life. Relationship is intended by God to be an experience that exposes us, transforms us, and mends us.

Too often, our culture tries to reduce love to a feeling. Love is so much more than a little ol' feeling. Love is the energy that created all of life. Love is the force that saved the world from sin. And love is the great power working to set things right again. That's the miracle of love. It is so powerful that it can transform even the most horrific events in our lives into something beautiful.[1]

Our desire for love, though derived from God and endowed by God, is not limited to God. We are made for relationship with the opposite sex, and this is expressed most clearly in romantic love. Relationships between men and women are a profound and powerful mystery created by God to reveal glory (both God's and our own), express character (both God's and our own), and give pleasure (to God and to us). But relationships between men and women often have more failure than success, more pain than pleasure, more hope deferred than hope fulfilled. This is what makes our relationships such a paradox.

When we are in love, we become our most vulnerable. When we enter a relationship without defensiveness, we have the opportunity for our deepest desires to be satisfied and our richest longings fulfilled. Romantic relationships expose our hearts and draw us out (to be present). To know and to be fully known by another is what life is all about. And when this happens, we get to know both sides, the good as well as the bad.

Romantic relationships expose the glorious parts in us and reveal the hideous effects of selfishness in our lives. Intimate relationships compel us toward gratitude and worship. They also move us toward confession and repentance. When we become willing to acknowledge how much harm we can do to another person by our sinful depravity, when we continuously endeavor to tell the truth about the effects of our worst impulses and respectfully seek amends and ask God to change our character defects (because we lack the power to change them ourselves), *only then* will we be transformed into more holy and humble men—more Christlike people.

Sadly, instead of letting our relationships change our hearts to reflect God's love, a lot of us guys look to our relationships with women as a way of validating our self-worth. We look to women (especially our mothers, wives, fiancées, or girlfriends) for affirmation, and to answer the question, Do I have what it takes?

Too often, for guys stuck in this pattern, romantic love becomes a fabricated relationship, or what Harry Schaumburg calls "a false intimacy."[2] Men make women, or sex, or both a conquest—a measuring stick for their masculinity. They end up using women so they can feel okay about themselves.

This can run the gamut from married guys to single guys. Take heed: Men who pressure or manipulate their wives into having sex are immature bullies at best, and more likely abusive jerks (whether they do it subtly or forcefully). This is only made worse when these guys are Christians because they take a sacred part of the marriage relationship and submerge it in shame and contempt, often in the name of spiritual leadership.

HOW TO TIE A TIE

For our purposes here, we will focus on the classic and most basic knot for neckties: the Windsor Knot. (Note: www.tie-a-tie.net offers pictures for each of these steps.)

1. With the tie draped around your neck under your shirt collar, the wide end should hang about twelve inches below the narrow end. Cross the wide end over the narrow end.

2. Bring the wide end up through the loop between the collar and your tie, then back down.

3. Pull the wide end underneath the narrow end and to the right, back through the loop and to the right again so that the wide end is inside out.

4. Bring the wide end across the front from right to left.

5. Pull the wide end up behind and through the loop again.

6. Bring the wide end down through the knot in front.

7. Using both hands, tighten the knot carefully and draw it up to the collar.

(If it's a bow tie, go to Brooks Brothers and let them coach you. . . . It's way too hard to explain.)

Adapted from www.tie-a-tie.net.

On the other end of the spectrum there are these single dudes of all ages who prey on women. These players are the guys who are most afraid of being exposed for who they really are: boys in wolves' clothing.

Whichever the guy, many a man turns the significant woman in his life into a goddess endowed with the power to define his self-worth. "If she's happy with me, then I'm okay. If she's not, then I'm a loser."

When relationship plays itself like this, it squelches authenticity and reduces relationship to being performance driven. In this scenario the best we can hope for is quid pro quo—tit for tat—where we exchange services with one another. I'll do this for you if you do this for me. We play nice but all the while build up a closet full of resentments. We may stay "happy" for a long time, but we move no closer to being the men God longs for us to be.

For a man to sail into the adventurous mystery of love, he must be willing to be vulnerable and emotionally generous, not manipulative and defensive. We're talking about the essential need for trust in our relationships with women.

How far can you be trusted with women? Are you emotionally safe, spiritually sensitive, consistent and dependable in action, and respectful, considerate, and honoring in the area of sexuality? Or are you aware that you intimidate and manipulate the opposite sex?

To the extent that you are trustworthy with the most significant woman in your life, there will be love. But many guys wrestle with shame and secrets that are barriers to trust (and, therefore, to love).

Dirty Laundry

Then there's the plague of pornography. Twenty years ago, a guy had to be pretty darn creative in figuring out how to sneak into a market or gas station and buy himself a copy of *Playboy* magazine. In today's culture, he doesn't even have to leave his own bedroom. He can access hundreds of sites in an hour's time. He can even get porn right on his cell phone.

Sex addiction is on the rise like no other time in history, so why are we so surprised? Our culture has immersed men in almost nonstop sexuality. (Just open any magazine, watch an hour of television, or listen to drive-time radio, if you're not convinced.) A lot of men have either seen or experienced sex in some of the most distorted and perverted ways possible. Due to all this sexual baggage, a lot of guys end up making a huge mess of things with the women they love.

Perhaps the most significant aspect of practicing the art of the fairer sex is understanding how our stories (the sum total of our life experiences) affect how we relate (or don't relate) with women. Many of us guys have gotten the wrong ideas about our relationships with women. We're confused about the proper role of sexuality in our relationships, and these flawed views lead to all kinds of resentment, shame, and conflict.

As counselors, we hear a lot from men on the issues of sexuality. Here are some glimpses into the lives of some men with whom we have spoken. You may recognize some pieces of your own story in a few of these.

> When **Joe** turned thirteen, his dad
> took him away for a "guys' weekend."
> As they were driving to their des-
> tination, Joe's dad made him listen
> to some tapes about sex and purity.
> Although they had never before talked
> about sex, the entire weekend was
> a call for Joe to "live pure" until his
> wedding night. As they returned home
> late Sunday night, Joe's dad gave him
> a new Bible, and they both prayed for
> Joe's future wife. Joe and his father
> never talked about sex again.

Riding the bus home from school one afternoon, eight-year-old **Timmy** was talking with his friends when a fifth grader turned around in his seat and asked the younger boys, "Do you want to know where babies come from?" Thus began a five-minute graphic and vulgar description of sexual intercourse, pregnancy, and delivery.

Chris's parents divorced when he was a young boy. After the separation, his dad moved to another state, and Chris lived with his mother and younger sister. When he was almost ten, his mother called him and his sister into the living room one day and read them a book she had gotten from the bookstore. She said they could ask questions whenever they wanted, about anything they wanted, and she would do her best to answer them. As Chris got older, there were many questions he had that he never felt comfortable asking his mom, so he kept silent.

When **Jim** was seven years old, his older brother took him to the house of a friend whose father owned pornographic movies. Young Jimmy watched the movies with much curiosity and fascination. On the way home, his brother said to him, "Now you know about sex. Don't tell Mom and Dad what we did."

Growing up, **Tom** spent three weeks every summer at his grandparents' farm in Wisconsin. When Tom was nine, his thirteen-year-old cousin Ron was visiting the grandparents at the same time. Ron was Tom's hero, and Tom followed him around day and night. One afternoon, Ron sexually abused his younger cousin in the barn and "taught" Tom about oral sex. He made Tom promise not to tell anyone their "special secret." Ron assaulted Tom regularly throughout his summer visit. Until recently, Tom had never told anyone.

Brian grew up on a farm in the country with his mom, dad, and younger brother. The entire family went to church together each Sunday morning, Sunday evening, and Wednesday night. Brian got along really well with his family. When Brian was about twelve, he was riding with his dad on the way to the co-op to get supplies for the farm. His dad, never turning to face him in the cab of the truck, just stared at the road and said, "Son, you need to know about sex. It's kind of like baseball. You have the ball, and the woman has the mitt. Do you have any questions?" Brian said, "No, sir."

For **Mark**'s sixteenth birthday, his parents handed him the keys to a fully refurbished 1968 Ford Mustang GT convertible. Mark was ecstatic. He and his dad jumped in to go for Mark's first ride. As they drove down the road, Mark's dad asked him to pull over in a parking lot. While there, Mark received another gift

from his dad—a pack of condoms—
with these fatherly words of advice:
"Son, now that you have your own
wheels, you'll be one of the big men
on campus. Just make sure you wear
one of these, so you don't get her
pregnant."

After two years of fighting for his
position, **Sam** was finally named
a first-string linebacker. Following
practice one day, as the team was
showering in the locker room, Sam
was toweling off when he became
sexually aroused. Many of his teammates noticed and whispered to
each other, laughing at Sam. In the
spring, Sam didn't attend the spring
practices and ultimately told the
coach he was quitting the team and
would not play his senior season. His
mom and dad supported his decision,
even though they never understood
why he quit. Sam still questions his
sexuality and often wonders if this
means he's gay.

Swept Clean

What happened to all the shame these guys experienced? It was swept under the rug. In truth, most of us have swept so much stuff under the rug in our lives that there's a bulging lump in the middle of the room—a filthy mound of deceit, betrayal, and compromise. Because of our pasts, we've become toxically ashamed of ourselves. We keep secrets. We tell ourselves, "If anybody knew this about me, they would reject me."

For too long, that is how I (Stephen) felt about much of my story. Much of my sexual education came from a variety of sources. Some were more legitimate than others. On the legitimate side, for example, my mom was really responsible about talking with me about sex from an early age, along with giving me age-appropriate books. My church youth group did a lot to encourage me and give me helpful—if not always biblical—information. And how could I forget Coach Coutras, my straightforward health teacher during my freshman year in high school. He didn't miss a thing, whether we wanted to know about it or not.

Then there's the illegitimate side. Like the day I found a stash of *Playboy* magazines at the base of a tree by the creek in our neighborhood when I was seven or eight. Or the time when a friend showed me pictures from an

HOW TO DELIVER A BABY

Okay, so your wife is in labor and you're on the way to the hospital. She's screaming, "Go faster! Faster!" Then, in the next breath, she shouts, "Slow down! Slow down! Quit hitting all the bumps in the road!" For good measure, she throws in, "Why did you do this to me?" It's becoming pretty clear that the baby is coming, and you're not going to make it to the hospital in time. What should you do?

Look guys, this one is very tricky. Let's really pray that we never have to actually do this on our own. But if, for some crazy reason, it does happen, remember this acronym: G.A.M.E. O.N.

Get help. Call 9-1-1 from your cell phone. Enlist the help of others passing by.

Assess the situation. Are there any problems you need to tell the EMTs when they get there? Like, is she having twins? Is the baby breech (coming out feet first)?

Maintain your composure. This is your chance to be a hero. Don't freak out. Childbirth is painful, loud, messy, and scary. Your primary role is to comfort and reassure your wife, no matter how nauseated you feel.

Encourage her. Talk to her. Tell her to breathe. If she feels like pushing, ask her to pant instead.

Open a jacket, blanket, or newspaper for her to sit on.

Now! Wait until the contractions are really strong and the baby is starting to come out (crowning). Your wife needs to push when contractions are strong and rest at other times.

When the baby's head comes out, cradle it in your hands and move it slightly downward as she pushes. (If the umbilical cord is wrapped around the head or neck, gently work it free.) Clear the baby's mouth of any obstructions. Help the shoulders to ease out one at a time. Once both shoulders are clear, the baby should slip right out like a greased watermelon. DON'T DROP THE BABY! Wrap the baby in a clean blanket or shirt and gently lay it on Mommy's chest. (Don't try to pull out the placenta. If it comes out on its own, wrap it in a newspaper or towel and keep it above the level of the baby's head until help arrives. Do not cut the umbilical cord.)

You did it, big boy. The EMTs should be there any moment. Keep mom and baby warm and dry.

Now, more realistically, let's talk about playing a supportive role at the hospital.

1. **READ OUR FIRST BOOK,** *BECOMING A DAD*. (Why wouldn't we recommend it?)

2. **HAVE A BAG PACKED WITH ALL THE ESSENTIALS AT LEAST A MONTH BEFORE THE DUE DATE.** (You just never know.)

3. **SAY THINGS LIKE, "I LOVE YOU."** "You're doing great." "You look beautiful." Repeat.

4. **GET SOME THICK SKIN, BOYS.** When labor kicks in, you are most likely going to get a verbal lashing of some kind. Don't take it personally.

5. **MAKE SURE YOU HAVE A CUP OF ICE SHAVINGS FOR YOUR WIFE TO BITE AND CHEW.** She's not allowed to eat.

6. **STROKE HER HAIR AND HOLD HER HAND.** If she says, "Get out of my face," get out of her face.

7. **PAY ATTENTION TO THE MONITOR SO YOU WILL KNOW WHEN THE CONTRACTIONS ARE COMING.** When they come, be ready and available for whatever she needs. Helping her know when a contraction is almost done and encouraging her are the best things you can do. But be prepared to shut your mouth, too.

8. **INTRODUCE YOUR WIFE TO HER CHILD.** Be the one to put that precious baby into her arms for the first time.

9. **DON'T WORRY WHEN YOU CHANGE THAT FIRST DIA-PER.** The poop (meconium) is supposed to look like tar.

Adapted from Joshua Piven and David Borgenicht, *The Worst-Case Scenario Survival Handbook* (San Francisco: Chronicle Books, 1999), 99–102; and Rod Brouhard, "To Deliver a Baby," http://firstaid.about.com/od/childbirth/ht/deliverbaby.htm; and Wade Meredith, "How to Deliver a Baby," www.healthbolt.net/2006/12/07/how-to-deliver-a-baby.

Internet bulletin board when I was in middle school. (This was way before the "www-dot" thing.) And then there was the day, when I was eleven or twelve, when I was left alone for several hours while everyone was out. Bored, I began nosing around the house, looking for something that might catch my attention.

I rifled through my sister's room, going through her dresser drawers, her closet, and her bathroom. I looked in all of the cabinets in the laundry room and rummaged around in musty coat closets and seldom-used storage closets. I was looking for anything that might hold my attention longer than ten seconds. After some time, I ended up in my parents' bedroom. Once I had snooped through all their drawers and looked under their bed, I began to explore their closet.

I poked around without success until I noticed a pair of my father's old boots on the top shelf. They were faded denim with tan leather trim. I got a stool and grabbed one. It weighed more than I expected, and I almost dropped it. When I looked inside, I discovered a handgun. It was a black metal revolver with a wood handle. I slid the gun out of the boot and handled it flat in my palm, measuring its weight. It was heavy and cold. I was scared and at the same time intensely fascinated. The house was so quiet that I could hear my heart thumping, full of excitement, fear, and shame.

The gun smelled oily and masculine, and though I had never held a weapon before, I knew what I had in my hands was powerful and dangerous.

After a few moments of aiming the gun around the closet, pretending I was Han Solo with his blaster, my fear compelled me to put the gun back where I found it. As I placed the dusty old boot on the shelf next to its mate, I noticed six or seven VHS cassettes. Curious, I examined the tapes to see what they were. Most were not labeled, and the ones that were marked had pieces of aging masking tape with faint, illegible script made in pencil. I took a few of the tapes down and went into the living room to see what I might find. Maybe old home movies, I thought.

I put a tape in the VCR and sat back on the couch. With the remote, I rewound the tape to the beginning. After a minute or two the tape came to a stop with a loud clunk. I pressed play, and there on our forty-eight-inch, big-screen color TV, was a scene of a man and a woman doing the deal. The graphic images and sounds that filled my brain—well, nothing was left to the imagination. I felt a weight sitting on my chest that pinned me to the sofa. Much like with the handgun a few minutes earlier, I was simultaneously frightened and enthralled. This was way more explicit than the centerfolds I had found by the creek bank or the flickering images that popped in and out on late-night cable TV.

The picture was grainy and the sound muffled, like the tape was a copy of a copy. But it didn't matter. I was experiencing levels of arousal I had not known (and shame I would not have imagined). I watched several minutes' worth of each tape before putting them back in their exact places on the shelf. Over the next several months, I returned to those tapes often, until one day they vanished—an empty space on the shelf where they once sat.

Sadly, what I learned from those tapes overshadowed much of the positive information I received. A lot of what I thought I knew about sex I got from pornography. My shame, and distorted expectations, plagued me for years.

The pervasiveness of pornography in American culture is staggering. Here are a few statistics that might help to put it in perspective:

- Number of pornographic Web sites: 4.2 million.
- People who regularly visit Internet porn sites: 40 million.
- Christians who said pornography is a major problem in the home: 47 percent.

- Porn revenue exceeds the combined revenues of all professional football, baseball, and basketball franchises.
- U.S. porn revenue exceeds the combined revenues of ABC, CBS, and NBC at $6.2 billion.[3]

There is a huge downside to all of this for men if we have learned about sex or were influenced in ways that are outside the categories of nobility, honor, trust, and respect. Our obscured vision of sex leaves us with shame, self-loathing, and contempt for others. That's why sex can be so difficult. That's why men (and women) sometimes wander away mentally during sex, or become addicted sexually, or masturbate regularly, or fantasize about someone else, or wish for it to just hurry up and end, or have affairs, or go to strip clubs, or struggle with same-sex issues, or do whatever else they can think up.

Somewhere along our journeys as men, our sexuality got linked with shame. In our refusal to face our pain and shame, we swept it under the rug. We've kept secrets, and it's these secrets that keep us from living fully. The only hope we really have is to roll up the carpet and expose our dirt so that we may experience the grace and freedom that could be ours.

If because of past heartache you've become disengaged, inattentive, abusive, or neglectful, both with others and with yourself, please read the next two sentences. If you've experienced sexual trauma in your childhood or adolescence (or even just have questions about it), *seek help*! If you're keeping secrets about your past or your present, find a safe place to tell them. Go to a qualified therapist, speak with a *wise* and *informed* pastor, attend a twelve-step meeting. Don't ignore the painful reality of your story and pretend that it doesn't affect how you relate to the woman in your life. The bravest thing you can do is to wrestle with God over the shame surrounding your sexuality.

Painting a Picture of Love

Our relationships with women are designed to be good. They're important to God. At its best, romantic love draws us to the throne of God, the place where we are most needy and most fulfilled at the same time. As designed by God, relationships between men and women are intended to reveal God's glory (and our glory). Thus, all of our relationships can be measured against two simple questions:

1. Where does this relationship embody God's love, magnificence, and righteousness, and where does it not?

2. Am I telling the truth about the first question, and am I willing to change in order to grow in wisdom and maturity?

C. S. Lewis may be most recognized today for writing the *Chronicles of Narnia*, but the story that was most influential in his life was that of his love for his wife, Joy. Lewis, who was a fiery apologetics professor at Oxford University, had an answer for everything until his faith was nearly extinguished when Joy died of cancer. In *A Grief Observed* (the book that inspired the film *Shadowlands*), Lewis reflects on his marriage and the pain of Joy's death. He writes, "Nothing will shake a man—or at any rate a man like me—out of his merely verbal thinking and his merely notional beliefs. He has to be knocked silly before he comes to his senses. Only torture will bring out the truth. Only under torture does he discover it himself."[4] If we open ourselves up to love, we risk the threat of pain. But if we don't, we run the risk of remaining immature. The struggle we must all face is whether to risk pain in order to gain maturity or to guard ourselves and remain foolish.

The art of engaging the fairer sex is about being aware of our power as men to bless the women in our lives with love, to recognize God's purpose in our relationships, and to see God's hand working to redeem the shameful or painful parts of our stories. As we become more adept at this, we will grow in our ability to paint a picture of love that will change not only our relationships with women, but also our families, our communities, and—dare we say it?—even the world.

Lessons Learned

1. *Middle school is about as close to hell as any of us have come.*
2. *Women are hard to figure out.*
3. *We need to unpack our sexual baggage.*
4. *Men have the power to bless.*

How to Move On from Here

How to move on from here? Well, the point is not so much to move on as it is to circle back, examine our stories, and make sure we're building on a solid, redeemed, and restored foundation. For starters, you can take stock of your female relationships—starting with your mom. Do you have her on a pedestal? Or do you villainize her? Was she Betty Crocker or Mommy Dearest? What was she like, and how has that affected your relationships with other women? Take the same inventory regarding your dad—or your father figure. How did he treat women? What did you absorb, both good and bad, about the art of engaging the fairer sex?

If you are struggling with sexual sin or sexual addiction, get help. Don't be a knucklehead and think you can resolve that kind of thing on your own. This is a serious problem for a lot of guys, and too many of them try to tackle this using only their own will-power. You need help. Check out programs in your area like Sexaholics Anonymous (SA), Celebrate Recovery, or the YMCA's Restore Ministry, or see a qualified counselor.

If your own camp is in order and you want to improve your communication with the woman you love, get a copy of a book we wrote called *Does This Dress Make Me Look Fat?: A Man's Guide to the Loaded Questions Women Ask.* (Okay, it's a shameless plug for our own product, but we believe you'll find it enlightening.) It won't solve all your problems, but it just might help you avoid some of the more common ones.

CHAPTER 4

Pop the Hood

The Art of Incompetence

I (David) fantasize about leasing a vehicle someday. I don't care what Dave Ramsey or Suze Orman says about how financially unwise it is. I know you don't have any equity . . . I know it's like flushing cash down the toilet . . . blah, blah, blah. I get it. I don't disagree with any of their logic, but what dear ol' Dave and Suze don't address is how sweet it would be to turn a vehicle back in once it reached 25,000 miles or so. The idea of owning a car that I never drove past its warranty would be a taste of heaven for me.

The fact of the matter is this: The warranty extends to 36,000 miles because nothing *ever* goes wrong before that point. The automakers can guarantee bumper-to-bumper coverage because they know you won't need to use it. And on the slight chance that you *do* need to take your car in, it'll be a minor deal, and they'll repair it on the spot. In twenty-two years of driving, I've only owned two cars that were still under warranty (for a short period of time), and the only warranty repair I've ever received was one time when the right rear blinker went out. The blinker!

The leasing fantasy is strong in me because I have a long history of owning vehicles that are so far out of warranty that it's only a distant memory. When I was a kid, we had a series of old cars. They always needed repairs, none of which were ever covered by a warranty. My dad loved cars and knew a lot about buying cars and comparing models, but he knew only the basics of car *maintenance* and *repair*. He knew just enough to survive and to be slightly more knowledgeable than a woman—changing the oil, replacing a flat, identifying a broken belt, things like that. I'm even less mechanically minded than my father. He passed on what knowledge he had (a percentage of which stayed with me), but I'm mostly fair game for auto mechanics (they love me!) because they can tell I don't really have a clue.

Furthermore, I think you either have a mechanical gift or you don't. Whatever color of brain matter (white, gray, turquoise, magenta) that makes a guy skilled in mechanics is missing in my noggin. I got an abundance of the other matter, I suppose. When I work on mechanically driven projects with my sons, I'll often remind them that men who write books, counsel other men, and have feelings can't also fix things. "It's virtually impossible," I say. This is, of course, not true, but it makes me feel better.

My grandfather was a contractor—an extremely well-respected builder, known for the quality and precision of his work. He's loaded with the right kind of brain matter. I'm his only grandson. He had five daughters, multiple granddaughters, and me. I'm certain he had hopes that I would someday take over his business. But then I worked for him one summer. I'd been on a job site for about two weeks when he made me promise that I would go to college and get a degree.

So here I am with a noggin full of nonmechanical, useless matter, and I live in a historic neighborhood, in a house built in the early 1900s, in which something breaks down or falls apart every ten to fifteen minutes, and I drive an old Volvo station wagon. By old, I mean that it was built decades ago, after I was born but before I got married. It has a gazillion miles on it. When you get above 55 mph on the interstate, it shakes and vibrates like it's gonna erupt and spill its parts all over the road. The hatch is broken, so you have to prop it on top of your head in order to load or unload anything. One of my sons kicked the back console hard enough that the back vent won't blow effectively, and the ashtray flies out from time to time. The driver-side fender is dented in where some yahoo backed into me in a parking lot and drove off. (Not enough to cause serious damage, but way too expensive to fix.) The rear windows won't roll down, and the driver's seat collapses on occasion when you attempt to crank it back. It only has two working positions—posture perfect or MacDaddy. When Mac-Daddy happens, I turn my ball cap sideways, roll the windows down (the few that work), and crank up the rap. And because it's a wagon, I call myself Ten Cents.

My first car at sixteen was a pale blue Datsun 210 wagon that we bought from my grandparents. It used to make me sick to my stomach to drive it on a date, but my parents just said, "Deal with it." So I named it the Blue Suppository. I had my first real wreck, my first speeding ticket, and my first flat in that car. Ahhh, the memories.

Some years after the Blue Suppository passed on, I inherited my dad's old Maxima, and my dad inherited his dad's 1950-something Ford Fairlane. The Maxima would overheat on the interstate between home and school, and periodically I'd have to have it towed. Then, one weekend, I was pulling into a fast-food joint, and the back axle collapsed. The rear half of the car was dragging on the ground. It was never the same after that.

Somewhere about that time, the state of Tennessee passed an environmental law requiring all drivers to pass an emissions test before renewing their tags.

Every year at renewal time, I would feel the tension because, although I was radically supportive of preserving and protecting the environment, my car was not. Ultimately, I think emissions testing is a good thing; however, for as long as this law has existed, at least one (if not all) of my vehicles has failed the test.

My friends who sell pharmaceuticals (or have some job besides working for a nonprofit) haven't had the humbling pleasure of being handed a failed emissions test score. They've never experienced driving toward the examiner, having the hose shoved up the car's exhaust, and begging Jesus for mercy. (I have had some of my most intimate encounters with Christ while in the hour-long emissions line.)

You see, when you fail, you get to drive your car to a service station and wait for several *more* hours while they assess your situation (and brainstorm over how much they can charge you). They know they've got you, because unless you pay them whatever they want for whatever they dream up is wrong with your vehicle, you're not going to pass the test, and you'll be driving on expired tags. And I'm amazed at how easily policemen can see that teeny tiny date on the two-inch sticker in the top right-hand corner of my license plate in the dark. It's astonishing.

One year, I failed the emissions test three times. I was

HOW TO DRIVE A STICK

Every guy needs to be able to drive a stick. There's just something uniquely masculine about shifting gears while you round a corner or pass someone on the road. Grab a friend with a little know-how, rent a manual transmission (don't ask your buddy to loan you his car, unless you don't value the friendship in the first place), and head to a mall parking lot after hours. It's just like riding a bike or motorcycle; you've got to get a feel for the art of shifting gears, and then you're on your way.

1. Use your left foot for the clutch and your right foot for the brake and gas pedal. Never hit the brake with your clutch foot. That's a bad combination. (If you've done this, you know what we mean).

2. With the car turned off, practice switching the gears—clutch, shift, gradual release. Then, on level ground, with the engine running and your left foot pressing the clutch, put the car in first gear. Slowly let the clutch out and simultaneously apply pressure on the gas pedal. (Doing this too quickly will squeal the tires, but please don't be that guy . . . even if you *are* a teenager. It really doesn't make you look cool.)

3. As you gain speed and the RPMs get beyond 2,000 or 3,000 (the tone of the engine will start to sound higher), push in the clutch, take your foot off the gas, and shift the stick from first to second gear. Repeat this procedure as you accelerate to the desired speed (or the posted

speed limit—whichever comes first). Use the same rhythm from high gear to low gear as you slow down.

4. Remember, never switch gears unless the clutch is pushed in. If you try, it will make an awful grinding sound. (By the way, that weird smell is the clutch burning up.)

Now you're ready to return the rental car and go buy the sports car or Jeep Wrangler you've always wanted.

in graduate school at the time, and Connie was teaching (we had little to no money). They gave me a certificate that said FAILED; and yes, it was in all caps. I drove straight to a service station that had a sign that read, "FAILED Emissions? We've got your solution." *Thank God,* I thought to myself. I pulled in, and a guy in a navy jumpsuit with a patch that read "Jared" walked out to meet me. "Let me guess, my brother, you failed emissions, didn't ya?" I wondered what gave it away . . . the piece of junk I was driving or the look of fury on my face. Or could he just smell those FAILED certificates coming from a mile away?

I gave a fake laugh and said, "You guessed it. Any chance you could take a look at it right now?"

"Oh no. Not right now. We're slammed this morning, but if you wanna leave 'er with us, we could get to it by this afternoon."

I was a good three miles from home, but my wife was teaching and couldn't leave work to pick me up, so I agreed to Jared's arrangement, gave him my contact information, grabbed my backpack, and started walking. I settled in at home and awaited his call. About two hours later, Jared called back and greeted me with, "Well, Mr. Thomas, it ain't lookin' good." You know, I can't recall ever having a conversation with a mechanic that didn't begin that way.

"You don't say, Jared. What seems to be the problem?"

He launched into a lengthy explanation about how cars of that age blah, blah, blah. I heard him out and said, "Cut to the chase, Jared. How much is it gonna cost me?"

"Well, there's where I've got some good news for ya, Mr. T." (Yeah, he called me "Mr. T.") "I can handle that problem for only $286, including labor, and I'll have her done for ya by 3 p.m."

"That's great, Jared. That's only two weeks of groceries for us. I'll walk back, bring you a check, and that'll give me time to go back through emissions before they close at five."

I wrapped up my work and headed out to reclaim my car. I paid Jared for his services and sped off to emissions, anxious to wrap this thing up. I got a different examiner this time, paid my fee (again), and didn't see the need to reconnect with my Savior for a second time at emissions. But I was wrong. The examiner yanked the stick out of my exhaust pipe and handed me another failed certificate.

"This is impossible," I barked. "I just had this car serviced not fifteen minutes ago, and he assured me it would pass emissions this time."

The examiner looked at me like a person does who has

absolutely zero job satisfaction. And who could blame her? Your job consists of ramming a stick up someone's muffler and smelling exhaust fumes all day. How could you possibly love what you do? She responded by saying, "Well, I'd march myself right back over there and give him a piece of my mind, that's what I'd do."

That was the best advice I'd gotten in weeks. And that's exactly what I did. Jared saw me coming and looked panicked that he'd already taken his lunch break and couldn't run and hide.

"Jared—" I shouted as I exited the car.

He interrupted me with, "Mr. T., I didn't expect to be seeing you again so soon."

"Well you *shouldn't* be seeing me again, but I failed emissions again. Again! After paying you two hundred and something dollars to fix this car!"

"Calm down, Mr. T. Back that thing over here, and I'll test her for ya." He had his own means of evaluating the exhaust. "I'm sorry, Mr. T., but I'm here to tell ya this car is satisfactory. Sat-is-fac-tor-y, I say. You drive this thing back over to emissions and tell them Jared's tested her out and somethin' ain't right." He spoke all this with the authority of a former president.

"Jared, they don't even know *who you are* at the emissions place. That won't mean anything to them."

"You show 'em that receipt I gave you. Give it back

to me. I'm gonna write 'em a note and tell 'em I tested it right here," he demanded as he frantically searched the passenger seat for the receipt he provided me earlier.

The crazy part of it all is that in that moment I actually bought into it. I was so desperate to pass emissions that I somehow believed that a note from the shop teacher would excuse me from detention. Looking back now, I think, *Dude, what were you thinking?* But sure enough, I left with his note and managed to get the same attendant from my second attempt at emissions. I read her badge this time and saw that her name was Lakisha. I called her by name and poured on the charm as I handed over Jared's receipt. "Lakisha, I just drove back to the service station, and Jared tested the car, and it passed. Can you believe that? He's written a note to verify that and has determined that nothing is unsatisfactory at this point."

Lakisha looked at me like I had just flashed her a membership card from the Lollipop Guild. She stared and said, "You kiddin', ain't ya?"

"No, I'm not kidding. He tested it himself and said it should have passed. Will you test it once more? You know how sometimes you get a false positive on a pregnancy test? And I may be in that small percentage today. Not pregnant obviously, but getting a false positive. Or in this case a false negative." My tone was now desperately close to begging.

She shifted her posture, folded her arms, and turned her attitude up about three notches. "Yeah, I'll test it again. You give me another ten bucks and I'll test it fifty times if you want me to, but it ain't wrong. Your mechanic is rippin' you off. And what's with him writin' a note? I don't care if Ronald Reagan sent you over here with a note. You ain't passin' emissions unless your car quits blowin' stuff out the back, you understand?"

I turned it up a notch myself. "I do. I do understand. But I shouldn't have to pay for a retest if I was just here ten minutes ago and there's a chance I got a false negative. Why else would I have come back this soon having had a mechanic say it's fine?"

"Did you hear what I said about ya note?" Lakisha asked.

"Lakisha, I'm not here to mess with your day. I just want to pass emissions. Please help me out," I asked, all while thinking I should know better than to pull into this place without requesting Jesus' presence.

"Oh, I'll help you out. Give me ten bucks and I'll help you out all day."

I was too tired to fight her any longer, so I yanked out my wallet and handed over another ten bucks to make this misery end. She took the money, rolled her eyes, walked to the back of the car, shoved the stick in the exhaust pipe, and asked me to hit the gas. I did as she requested, then took my foot off the pedal when prompted and awaited the verdict. She ripped the certificate off the printer, sauntered over to me and said, "Well, tell Mr. Reagan that he needs to check his machine to see what seems to be the problem, because you failed *again*."

I was near tears by this point. "Okay, here's the new deal. I'll give you whatever amount of money you want to print me off a passing certificate. I know it's bribery," I pleaded as I reached for my wallet, "but I can't do this anymore."

Lakisha laughed and said, "You can't bribe me. Our government is corrupt, but it ain't that corrupt. Drive back over there and get your wallet out. The mechanic'll take your money."

I sped out in a fury and arrived just as Jared was closing up shop. He rolled his eyes at the sight of me. I was exiting the car before I had completely put it in park. I told Jared about my exchange with Lakisha and demanded that he figure out what the problem was. He told me to pull it back in front of the garage and he'd take another look. He popped the hood, and we both stared inside. It was covered over with oil and leaves and dirt and the corrosion of time. The belts all looked worn and tired. The battery looked about thirty-six years old, and all the other parts (none of which I could accurately identify) seemed to stare at me tauntingly. "You don't know our names. You don't have a clue."

I just stood and stared. Guys do that a lot. I suppose we feel empowered to have at least popped the hood and looked around. Like the parts might take pity on us and repair themselves. What was mostly foreign to me was deeply familiar to Jared. My incompetence was magnified by his knowledge and experience, and it made me hate him even more.

I felt even greater contempt when he agreed to stay late and figure out what was wrong. Jared recommended I take a seat inside and let him consider all the options. He knocked around for a while, and I called my wife to relay the emissions saga.

Failing emissions was like going to the optometrist. Just something we do once a year. She wasn't surprised to hear the beginning of the story, but grieved to hear the ending. She offered to come pick me up, but I told her I thought Jared would be wrapping things up shortly.

Jared replaced a couple of other things, flushed out the fuel tank, charged me more money, and tested it again (it passed). And I went home. Emissions was closed by now. I went back the next morning and ended up in the line next to Lakisha's station. I hollered out to her just after I hollered out to Jesus, and she looked over at me, visibly relieved that one of her colleagues would be dealing with me today (and any notes I might have brought back with me).

Somehow I passed. I don't know if Jared fixed the problem or if the computer is programmed to offer up a "pity pass" on your third attempt. Either way, I received my certificate and took it to the county clerk's office, where I stood in line for over an hour. By the time I reached the front of the line, I'd spent who knows how many hours and $623.86, including the cost of renewing the tags, getting to this point. I thanked Jesus for getting me there, Al Gore for initiating the emissions law, and Penny for taking my check.

I can't decide what's worse: the money I spend in obtaining the tags, the hours spent camped outside the emissions office, county clerk's desk, and Jared's service station; the anguish I experience over having no magenta brain matter to handle my own car maintenance; or the fact that I lack enough income to *lease a new vehicle!*

My leasing fantasy is ultimately about futility. Escaping futility is a consistent theme in life. It's one that God continues to reintroduce again and again (an obvious indicator that it hasn't yet sunk in). If it's not my

HOW TO CHANGE THE OIL
IN YOUR CAR

Do you enjoy tinkering around the garage? Do you own your own hand tools? Are you okay with getting a little grease under your fingernails? If your answer is yes to all of the above, you'll save roughly a hundred dollars a year by changing the oil in your cars yourself. Oh, and you'll save maybe another ten bucks by not having the guy at the quick-lube place sell you a $5.00 air filter for $14.95.

But if the thought of changing the oil yourself doesn't appeal to you, go to Jiffy Lube or Grease Monkey or your local quick-lube shop, shell out the thirty bucks, and be done with it. (Who are we kidding? Are we seriously interested in learning how to change the oil to maybe save $100 a year?) Changing the oil requires about twelve different things and fifteen steps. Besides, how many of you have a 3/8-drive socket set? How many of you even know what that is?

Exactly!

Listen guys, don't worry about this one. Just get the oil changed every five thousand miles and you'll be fine. (They want you to think you need to do it every three thousand, but it's a scam.)

Now, if you're really interested in changing your own oil, you probably already know how to do it, and you definitely don't need our advice.

house or my car, it's my family. I'm convinced it's part of why God gave me the "gift" of twins.

My daughter was fourteen months old when we discovered at an ultrasound that my wife was pregnant with twins. It would have been way too perfect for me to have had two children, one girl and one boy. Instead, God gave me three. Three car seats wouldn't fit in either one of our vehicles. Our tiny two-bedroom house at the time wasn't big enough for three children, and my salary wasn't enough to feed a family of five. Since our family has grown, nothing has worked. Almost, but not quite. And therefore, I end up at the end of myself over and over and over again.

That's exactly how God designed it to be, from the beginning of time. In the Genesis account, following the serpent's deception, Eve's eating the fruit, and Adam's silence, God addresses each of the parties involved. The serpent finds out he'll spend life on his belly, eating dust and waiting for his head to be crushed. Eve finds out that childbirth will be agonizing and she'll be stuck longing for a man who'll end up ruling over her. And then God lowers the boom on Adam. His consequence is double in length compared to Eve's.

> "Cursed is the ground because of
> you; through painful toil you will eat

of it all the days of your life. It will produce thorns and thistles for you, and
you will eat the plants of the field. By
the sweat of your brow you will eat your
food until you return to the ground,
since from it you were taken; for dust
you are and to dust you will return."[1]

The initial portion of the curse explains that men
will experience a sense of futility. Everything we do is
intended to be hard. It's designed to be difficult. The
second portion reveals that there will always be blood,
sweat, and tears. We will labor and labor and labor. And
we'll experience defeat. We'll be at war with the world,
and ultimately the world will win. The world is rigged
to defeat us and break us down. And here's the kicker:
God is the one who rigged it.

We'll experience futility in the work of our hands
and in the desires of our hearts. The car will continue
to break down, and we'll continue to fail emissions.
We'll continue to pop the hood, and we'll continue
to feel incompetent. Relationally, we will continue to
pursue our wives and children, and despite our best
intentions, we will continue to harm, fail, and disap-
point them. As husbands and fathers, our primary sense
of futility will occur with our wives and children, who

are also the source of our greatest joy. How's that for good news?

The good news comes in acknowledging that we're incapable of reversing the circumstances. Yet we continue to operate as if we can reverse the outcome. That's why bookstores are packed full of Seven Habit books, Ten Principles to This and That, and guaranteed ways to achieve success. We still believe we can avoid futility.

The reality is that freedom can only be found in surrender: surrender of the idol of mastery. We can't reverse the circumstances. We can, however, experience relationship with the same God who rigged this arrangement. We can live in communion with the one who is both the builder and the wrecking ball. In doing so, we experience more than just pain and futility; we experience forgiveness and redemption.

It's not about mastery. It's about mystery and surrender. It's futility giving way to dependence. It's allowing our hearts to be changed.

Resistance Is Futile

Like David, I (Stephen) am useless when it comes to the automotive arts. I barely know a lug nut from a peanut. I don't remember my dad handing down his vast knowledge about cars, and I doubt it would have mattered. Whatever the gene is that makes someone car savvy, I don't have it. I'm as clueless as Colonel Sanders at a wiener roast. There is a lot I don't know—like the time I put brake fluid in my washer fluid reservoir. Or the fact that for a long time I thought that a catalytic converter had something to do with Cadillacs, and for the life of me, I couldn't understand why my Mitsubishi had one. (And I still don't know what it does.)

I have tried to tell myself that my masculinity isn't measured by my knowledge of cars, but it hasn't worked all that well. The other day at a coffee shop, I overheard two gearheads talking about horsepower, torque, air dams, differentials, and camshafts. I felt like such a wimp, sitting there with my MacBook and a 2 percent, decaf latte. Nothing exposes my incompetence as a man quite like car talk.

When something goes wrong with my car, I procrastinate taking it to the mechanic, for fear that my lack of knowledge will betray me and I'll get charged double for whatever's wrong, simply because I don't know any better. And when I do take the car in, my wife always wants to know what the mechanic said, and why it will cost so much, and why it broke. Out of my shame, I try to explain, but I end up just feeling more stupid. "I don't know. The guy just said so."

In our self-esteem-driven culture, shame gets a bad rap. But shame has an upside, too. Shame is the emotional experience that tells us we can't do everything. It's the feeling that reminds us that we're not God. Healthy shame tells us, "You're not God, and neither is the other guy." The nature of shame is that it exposes our humanity, dependence, and imperfections. When we allow ourselves to embrace the experience of shame, we discover its gift: humility.[2]

The problem for many of us men is that we get scared when shame reveals our incompetence. We've been taught that real men don't show weakness. We've bought into the Superman myth. We wrongly believe that our worth is based in our production or what we have to offer. Shame is a terrifying experience for any man who has been taught to base his self-worth on his performance or his behavior. When we keep score, we end up harboring resentments, nursing grudges, and becoming bent on vengeance. Our healthy shame becomes toxic.

A lot of guys were raised in an environment that told them they had to earn love or that they would only get attention for what they accomplished. We recite mantras like "try harder," "winners never quit," "second is first loser," "only the strong survive," and "succeed or die trying."

When we live our lives based on what others think about us, we wear ourselves out trying to seek their approval or win their affection. The bar is always just a little higher than we can jump. Such performance-based living is a death sentence. We make ourselves sick trying to keep up or prove ourselves worthy of love. Living like this will ultimately kill us. This toxic shame is our condemnation of ourselves for being human.

Whenever our toxic shame is exposed, the toxicity intensifies. The nature of toxic shame is that it is only manageable when we keep it hidden; but when exposed, its poison is released. Toxic shame is like cow dung. The more the sun shines on it, the more it stinks.

Most of our toxic shame comes from the secrets we try to keep. Many guys have secrets that they don't want anybody else to ever know about. It's like we carry a bucket of vomit around our necks and try to convince people, through our hard work, acts of kindness, good looks, intellect, or whatever else, that we smell great.

Along with our secrets comes a voice that whispers, "What if somebody finds out?" When our self-image is infected with toxic shame, we believe that if somebody really knew us, they would reject us, harm us, or abandon us. We don't truly trust that anyone else is for us—especially God. Toxic shame causes us to live in fear, and it's this fear that then fuels our lives.

Instead of being energized by our passions, we live on the fuel of toxic shame. The resulting emotional flatulence is just as deadly as the shame itself. It pollutes our lives in one of three ways: contempt for ourselves, contempt for others, or contempt for both ourselves and others.

Self-contempt (which is just another way of saying *self-hatred*) occurs when our toxic shame is exposed. Here's what it often sounds like: "Why did I do that?" "How can I be so stupid?" "Something must be wrong with me [for needing others' approval or love or acceptance]." Self-contempt compels us to try to find an external resource to quiet the pain of our exposed shame. Often, it turns to lust. We lust for sex, money, power, fun, drugs, escape, TV, or whatever.

Contempt for others is an expression of shame that says, "I hate you." Often when our shame is exposed to someone else, we become filled with rage. Because we are terrified of being rejected on the basis of our revealed hearts, we choose to act in ways that will destroy or control whatever (or whoever) has exposed us. This other-centered contempt leads us to kill, erase, negate, shame, minimize, judge, or deny the presence of others because he or she has either exposed our shame or has seen our shame exposed. This is what Jesus is referring to when he says, "Anyone who is angry with his brother will be subject to judgment."[3] Other-centered contempt is the heart of murder.

When we combine the two (self-contempt and other-centered contempt), we get in real trouble. The

HOW TO HOT-WIRE A CAR

We know. We know. You would never do this. But every time you watch a TV show and some dude hot-wires a car, you know you wish you knew how. So here you go. Just make sure you hot-wire your own car and steer clear of a felony.

The following method takes more time than ripping and cutting up wires and panels, but it avoids damaging the car's interior.

Before you start, heed this little warning: Live wires carry a significant charge and can give you a painful shock. Touch only the insulated part of the wire and wear insulated gloves, if possible.

1. Locate the ignition tumbler, the spot where you normally put your key. Remove the covers and panels around the tumbler.

2. Examine the ignition setup. There should be a panel with five to eight wires clipped to the rear of the tumbler. Remove the panel and try to manually turn the ignition switch using a screwdriver. (If you can do this, you're done!)

3. If you are not able to manually turn the ignition switch with a screwdriver, you will have to strip some wires to hot-wire the car.

4. Locate the "on" positive and negative wires in the steering column. They should run up to the ignition tumbler and be color-coded. Pull those wires from the ignition,

strip a portion of each, and twist them together. The car will now be on and ready for ignition. This is where you truly hot-wire a car. Be careful: These wires carry a charge, which is why they are called "hot."

5. Find the starter wires and pull them from the ignition tumbler as well. Strip the ends and touch these wires together briefly. This should activate the starter, firing up the car. If you have done everything properly, your car will now be running. Do not leave these wires touching each other once the car is running. Cover up any exposed wires to avoid painful electric shocks.

6. Just because the car is running, it doesn't necessarily mean you can drive the car. Many cars have a steer-ing-wheel lock hooked into the ignition tumbler as an antitheft device (so you cannot unlock the steering wheel without the key). But hey, you succeeded in hot-wiring the car, so quit complaining.

Just so we're clear: These instructions are provided strictly for fun. We bear no responsibility if you mess up your ignition. And if you're dumb enough to try this on some random car, we will *not* visit you in jail.

Adapted from "How to Hot-Wire a Car," www.ehow.com/how_2044915_hotwire-car.html.

hatred we carry for ourselves and take out on others is a dangerous cocktail that ultimately leads to a hatred of God. As we practice rejecting our neediness and lusting for an external solution, we come to despise the very person who made us the way we are—God. In our contempt for God, we grow arrogant. We come to hate our neediness and incompetence. Any man who projects self-importance is really compensating for a deep level of toxic shame. He hates himself. He hates others. And he hates God. To compensate, he is left only to create a narcissistic reliance on his own strength. He becomes his own god, turning to pride, cockiness, or conceit as a way of managing his shame.

Inoculation for Toxic Shame

The antidote for toxic shame and the effects of contempt is love. The power of authentic relationship is that we are accepted *because* of our incompetence, not in spite of it. We are not made to be interdependent. We are not made to be codependent. We are not made to be independent. We are made to be dependent on others and God.*

In authentic community, a willingness to change

---

* Perhaps you have the same question our editor asked us: Isn't dependence on others the same as interdependence? (If I'm depending on them and they're depending on me . . .) But in fact they are not the same. *Interdependence* includes the idea that we lean into each other—we trade services. *Dependence* has to do with a deeper powerlessness—an awareness of our individual ability and a surrendering to the power of another.

is the only prerequisite for membership. (And the willingness doesn't even have to be totally sincere at first.) One central reason why groups like Alcoholics Anonymous, Narcotics Anonymous, Samson Society, Celebrate Recovery, and Sexaholics Anonymous work in delivering people from the death of toxic shame, contempt, apathy, depression, anxiety, and addictive disease, is that they are committed to accepting people where they are.

It's in places like these that we often discover an acceptance of ourselves as human—as people in need. The sad reality is that many secular recovery-centered groups are far more willing to invite, receive, and embrace the broken, needy, awkward, messy, incompetent, and smelly people of the world than are most Christian church congregations. The great majority of churches send unspoken messages that tell people, "Unless you meet a certain standard or expectation, you are not welcome." The gold standard in far too many churches reads something like this: If you can cover your stench, pretend that life really isn't that difficult, deny your doubts about God's goodness, minimize your sin, ignore that you have problems, and beat yourself up for not being quite perfect or good enough, then you, too, can belong.

The most scandalous thing about the message of

Jesus isn't that we have to trust that he is the Messiah. The most shocking thing about Jesus' life, death, and resurrection is that it frees us from trying to earn God's love. There is nothing we can do that will make God love us any less. And there is nothing we can do to make God love us more. He already loves us fully, completely, and absolutely.

Our ability to tolerate heartache, difficulty, and despair is mind-boggling. Until the pain of holding on to our secrets is worse than the fear of surrendering control, we will not change. It's only those who are willing to step out of hiding and expose their incompetence who will find freedom. When a man steps beyond his fear of rejection and into an authentic relationship with Christ, what he often experiences is the energizing rejuvenation of grace, the reassuring embrace of mercy, and the astounding recognition of acceptance.

The combination of grace, mercy, and acceptance is a concoction that God uses to set us free. But many Christian churches gave up their corner on the market of this type of community a long time ago. In its place, we now have guilt trips, toxic shame, and exclusion far too often. Getting people to do the right thing has become more important than living together in dependence on God. Most Christians are experts at hiding their distrust of God and others.

It's only the most desperate men who are willing to give up control over their present circumstances, deflate their egos, and expose their neediness in order to take the risk that things might be different. All of us want change, but few of us are willing to lay down our own agendas about how things need to be done and let God do for us what we can't do for ourselves. We are unwilling to be known fully, live with powerlessness, and expose our ineptitude.

Failure Is an Art Form

To practice the art of incompetence, we must learn to be confessional, repentant, and dependent. We must learn to embrace (and even love) failure. The art of incompetence is learning to succeed at being a failure.

Confessional living requires that we be gut-level honest in three ways: (1) with ourselves about ourselves; (2) with trustworthy others about ourselves; (3) and with God about ourselves. We must fess up to what is happening inside us—both the good and the bad.

Very often, men hold back in relationships by only reporting their behaviors. Less often, we tell the whole truth of our hearts—our attitudes, motives, and perspectives about ourselves, others, and God. This is why doing the "accountability partner" thing so often fails to accomplish what we hope it will. We don't know how, or we are unwilling, to really tell each other what is going on deep in our hearts.

The nature of confession is love (not shame). This is what James is getting at when he counsels us to "confess your sins to each other."[4] Confession is the willful exposure of our inner selves to someone else. Confession is intimacy. It draws us near to another person. And not only does confession bring us closer to other people, it also allows them to speak into our lives with accuracy, tenderness, and strength.

True confession always opens the door to repentance. Once our darkness is exposed to others, the only things left to feel are guilt, sorrow, and remorse. Confession that leads to repentance promotes a willingness to turn from our controlling, inauthentic, rage-filled, or medicating behavior toward a God who loves us and who longs to return us to wholeness. The nature of repentance is hoping that in our reaching out, God will change us or meet us or rescue us or care for us. Repentance creates a momentum toward surrender and powerlessness.

By recognizing our increasing need and our inability to live without support, input, and direction from God and others, we begin to live more fully in the mystery of the gospel and begin to discover the power of a loving God. In that way, the nature of dependence is faith—the bedrock of authentic Christianity.

This combination of confession, repentance, and dependence is the act, energy, and process that God uses to transform, heal, and mature us into being more of who we were made to be. Living out of our incompetence is a significant first step in living more fully as men.

Lessons Learned

1. *Futility is inescapable.*
2. *Shame can be a gift.*
3. *Toxic shame will make you your own god.*
4. *Authentic relationship is what we need.*

How to Move On from Here

Let's face it, stuff breaks and things don't always work out the way we want. What's a guy to do? Here's a suggestion: Read Genesis 3:17-19. Then reread it until the message is fully rooted in your heart. Tape it to your forehead, if necessary, to help you remember that futility is inevitable, but mistakes and failure, while they can change your life forever, don't have to define you.

It's also really important to identify how self-contempt rears its head in your life. In what ways do you discount your worth to others? How do you keep others from depending on you, or being interested in you, or being concerned about your fate? Do you deflect compliments? Do you not ask for help when you need it? Do you disbelieve someone's encouraging words for you? Do you feel sorry for yourself?

Toxic shame, the root of self-contempt, always originates in the family from which you came. Often, it is helpful to sit with a counselor or meet with a qualified pastor to help you begin to unpack how the wounds from your family of origin influence the level of toxic shame you feel.

CHAPTER 5

Bringin' Home the Bacon

The Art of Work and Rest

The 1989 film *Say Anything* is the tale of Lloyd Dobler's summer quest for love and meaning. Following high school graduation, Lloyd (a young John Cusack) forgoes the party-hearty escapades of his peers and embarks on a search for something more fulfilling. This pursuit leads Lloyd to confront his own desires for intimacy, identity, and purpose. In a memorable soliloquy, Lloyd expresses his vocational aspirations (or lack of them) to his prospective girlfriend's father.

> A career? I've thought about this
> quite a bit, sir, and I would have to
> say considering what's waiting out
> there for me, I don't want to sell
> anything, buy anything, or process
> anything as a career. I don't want
> to sell anything bought or processed;
> or buy anything sold or processed;

or repair anything sold, bought, or
processed as a career. I don't want to
do that. My father's in the army. He
wants me to join, but I can't work for
that corporation. So what I've been
doing lately is kickboxing, which is a
new sport . . . as far as career longev-
ity, I don't really know. I can't figure it
all out tonight, sir, so I'm just gonna
hang with your daughter.[1]

Lloyd sees the emptiness of just working his life away
without meaning. He's hungry for more. He wants to
be himself—at all costs. He knows he must go to work,
but his ambivalence about this reality puts him in a
bind. Lloyd can see that what the world calls work,
though necessary for survival, is often banal, painful,
and alienating. But unlike his party-focused friends,
Lloyd faces his quandary head-on. He risks disappointment by entering the mystery of the unknown and
banking on love, rather than resigning his efforts to an
existence focused on "selling, buying, or processing."

Have you ever thought that this work thing ain't all it's
cracked up to be? Have you ever said to yourself, "There
has to be more to life than an honest day's labor"?

Most of our lives are spent doing one of two things:

working or sleeping. In between those two, we try to squeeze in some other important stuff, like family, friends, service, faith, exercise, etc. Because there's not a whole lot we can do when we're sleeping, the time we spend working is probably pretty important in the grand scheme of things. To live fully as men means that how, why, and when we work must be taken into account. Becoming skilled at the art of work and rest is at the core of our becoming authentic men.

Rightly or wrongly, work provides us much of the meaning and purpose we find in life. Another way of saying this is that we don't really get to know all that much about ourselves, others, and God by sitting on our duffs. We're designed to experience, grieve, desire, build, fail, hope, create, risk, struggle, and dream. We're designed to move our fannies in the quest for full and rewarding lives.

These days my (Stephen's) dad is a golfer, but when I was growing up he was a salesman. He worked really hard to provide all that we needed and much of what we wanted. He was very successful at his work and did it with integrity. I remember him taking me on some of his sales calls and how warmly he was received. He obviously served his customers well, and they held him in high regard. He really lived by a motto that said, "If you treat people right, they will treat you right."

Probably the earliest childhood memory I have is concerning my father and work—well, kind of. I was with my mother in the threshold of our foyer. She was sitting, and I was standing in her lap—my bare feet pressed into her legs—so I could see out the glass pane of the front door. We were waiting for my father to get home from a business trip. He traveled a lot.

It was dark, and the sky glowed navy and gray as summer storm clouds gradually filled the sky over our neighborhood. My mother had turned off the lights in the front part of the house so that the only illumination came from the flickering gaslight in our front yard and a nearby streetlight that gave off just enough of an amber glow to cast shadows across the yard.

The lightning from the storm danced and flashed in the sky over the houses across the street and beyond. My hands and face were pressed hard against the lower glass pane, and I could feel the door rattle as the thunder shuddered the thin, aluminum storm door. I stared down the street, watching intently for my father's headlights to pierce the darkness and lead him into our driveway.

As the storm grew, I could tell that my mother was becoming more anxious. But even though it was dark and raining, I felt safe standing in her lap with her arms wrapped around my waist to steady me. I was full of anticipation of my father's return. And every few minutes, my hopes would rise and fall as another car came over the hill and continued on past our house . . . false alarm after false alarm.

For me, the pervasiveness of my father's absence is the most evident part of the memory. I wasn't scared or sad. It was lonely, I guess—lonely, like a boy for his father. The nearest thing I can acquaint it with is the emotional gap I feel whenever one or two of my kids spend the weekend at a grandparent's. You can just tell that someone's missing. Things seem unsettled.

I didn't know how many of my childhood memories were framed around my father's departures and arrivals until recently, when I was confronted by my own children.

I came into the living room from getting dressed the other day, and my four children were playing on the floor together. One of my two-year-old twins looked up at me and asked, "Dada go work?" It was a Saturday, and I wasn't going anywhere. I realized in that moment how often my older kids also ask me if I'm on my way out the door. Over time, these questions have become like punches to my kidneys. It hurts how often I hear that phrase, "Dada go work?" It seems right now that my children are more used to my leaving than any other experience of me. As with my own father, a majority of my children's moments with me are framed by my comings and goings. It seems I'm always in some state of transition with my kids.

The lesson really hit home when, after a couple days off work, I had spun down enough internally to realize how lonely I was for my family. My kids kept asking me when I was leaving. They kept looking at me with a look on their faces that said, "When are you going to work? What are you doing at home?" It was really quite tragic.

I began to see that I really don't have a good concept of the art of work and rest. I'm learning that I work far too much and rest far too little. As I consider this more deeply, I am beginning to see how out of whack I keep my life. When I see how distant I am from my family, I see how really distant I am from God.

But here's the tension, which I'm sure you've also felt: The role I play as provider is the very thing that requires me to leave the people I love the most. To engage my world through work, as many men do, requires me to leave my home and on some level, abandon my place with my family. It involves my leaving my wife and children to provide for what they need. There's something not quite right in that equation.

When it comes to the battle of work and rest, many men choose work over family. They begin a passionate love affair with their vocation. Work becomes like a mistress. She is seductive; she provides all kinds of confirmation, recognition, and financial gains; and she's all-consuming and always available.

Men leave home every day to work with their God-given talents to contribute to the families they've been given, and the tragedy is that it requires them to *leave* in order to do it. Like we mentioned earlier, the curses from the account of the Garden of Eden make it clear that the work we do will break our backs—and it will also break our hearts.

Free Falling

Labor has always been a means by which God teaches us about ourselves and about himself. This side of Eden, any effort will wear us out and leave us empty and hopeless. Apart from God doing it for us, we will be tired.

One verse in the Bible puts it like this: "Faith without works is dead."[2] Our doings don't define us; they reveal what is true about us. We're made by God to *be*, and being always compels us toward doing. Our actions expose the substance of our hearts.

Right from the beginning of Scripture (Genesis 1, 2, and 3), we see the centrality of labor to our understanding of ourselves, others, and God. The Bible makes it clear that God, too, is at work.

God formed the man from the dust
of the ground and breathed into his
nostrils the breath of life, and the man
became a living being. Now the LORD
God had planted a garden in the east,
in Eden; and there he put the man
he had formed. And the LORD God
made all kinds of trees grow out of the
ground—trees that were pleasing to
the eye and good for food. . . . Now
the LORD God had formed out of the
ground all the beasts of the field and
all the birds of the air. He brought
them to the man to see what he would
name them.[3]

Look at what's going on here. God formed, he breathed,
he planted, he put, he made, he formed again, and he
brought. Wow! God is one very busy dude.

In the book of Ephesians, the apostle Paul talks about
God's secret plan that has been in effect since before the
dawn of time.[4] And God's not done. Hebrews points
out that God has planned something better for us even
yet.[5] This picture of God is a far cry from that of a
wind-the-clock-and-walk-away, hands-off God. The

God of the Bible is not a deist; he is personally, actively at work in and through his creation.

As God's image bearers, we will come to know God and resemble God through our work. Christians are called "God's fellow workers."[6] We are to labor with him, in service to him, as he is in service to us.

But we're not laboring merely for labor's sake; rather, our labor is an expression of worship. Jesus said it this way: "If you follow me, you will have a cushy job."[7] Well, actually he said, "My yoke is easy and my burden is light,"[8] but you get the idea. Jesus says if we follow him, our labor with him will become a place of rest for our souls. Through Christ, the futility of the Curse is redeemed in our daily lives—in how we work, which is to say *worship*.

Work as worship. That's an extremely important concept for us to get. As Christians, we need to stretch our heads and hearts around the idea that worship is expressed in *everything* we do, not merely in the songs we sing on Sunday morning. The idea that worship takes place mostly on Sunday mornings is, well, anti-Christian. The term *worship leader* could be used for any Christ follower who has influence on others: from a parent to a CEO to a bus driver to a reporter. Anyone who interacts with anybody is, in truth, engaged in leading worship.

HOW TO INTERVIEW FOR A JOB

Effective motivational speakers have a savvy way of "reading the audience's mail." It's as if they can look at a crowd and say, "I know you." Inevitably, the crowd leans forward because they want to be known, and the speaker connects to this natural, human desire.

When you go for a job interview, think of yourself as the motivational speaker and the company you're interviewing with as the crowd. You want to "read the company's mail" during the interview. You want the interviewer to be thinking, *This guy really knows us!* If you are able to do this effectively, the interviewer will lean forward and consider you "the fit" he or she has been looking for.

How do you "read the company's mail"? Here are some quick tips:

1. **AVOID POSING.** Be true to who you are. If you don't know an answer to a question, tell the truth. There's no such thing as an expert. Nobody knows every single thing there is to know about any one subject. Sure, they may want you to be knowledgeable, but they're not expecting omniscience.

2. **BE PREPARED.** Be ready to answer the classic interview questions: strengths/weaknesses, passions, experience, a little bit about yourself, what separates you from the other applicants, and so on. Be prepared to *briefly* describe the specific personal achievements that you want the interviewer to remember.

3. **PERSONALIZE THINGS.** Make things as personal as you can. If you have any connections, *casually* drop a name. It's sad but true that it's not always *what* you know but rather *who* you know.

4. **DO YOUR HOMEWORK.** Research the organization and the culture. Understand the company's history, purpose, mission statement, product line, company size, major problems, programs, needs, etc.

5. **SEE TOMORROW.** If you are interviewing for a particular job, know what you would do to grow the position if hired. Interviewers love self-starters who have a vision and a plan to get there.

6. **TURN THE TABLES.** Interview the company based on your previous research. This makes you look knowledge-able and confident. Wouldn't it be great if a few companies were competing for your services?

7. **DRESS FOR SUCCESS.** Think first impressions. Look the interviewer in the eye and give a firm (but not aggressive) handshake. Dress appropriately for the job for which you are interviewing. Your appearance should make the interviewer think, *This person will fit in well.*

Adapted from Carole Martin, "What Are Your Greatest Strengths and Weaknesses?" http://career-advice.monster.com/job-interview-practice/What-Are-Your-Greatest-Strengths-an/home.aspx; and John Rossheim, "Do Your Homework Before the Big Interview," http://career-advice.monster.com/interview-preparation/Do-Your-Homework-Before-the-Big-Int/home.aspx; and Perri Capell, "How to Interview for a Job Without Raising Suspicions," www.careerpath.org/columnists/qanda/interviewing/20071226-qandainterviewing.html.

You see, it's not a question of are we worshiping something; rather, it's a question of *what* are we worshiping?

Does our work reflect God's creativity, mercy, justice, service, sacrifice, and love?

Or is our labor all about personal gain, acclaim, recognition, and security?

God's not looking for our payback. He gives to us freely. He's not a capitalist. He's far from it. God does not function on the principles of supply and demand or quid pro quo. He does not do for us once we have done for him. Through Jesus, God has already done for us more than we could ever repay. In fact, if you think about it, God paid a really inflated price for what he bought back. He traded in the perfect (Jesus) for the imperfect (the rest of us). Our work/worship is not about repaying a debt; it's a reply of gratitude for what God has done.

It's as if God were saying, "Forget the sacrifices and all the hard work. You can't pay me back. You can't stay even with me. Whatever you give me, I will give you more. I will give you everything you need and then some. You just have to let me love you."

God is like the host of the best Thanksgiving Day dinner you could ever imagine, prepared by the best cooks that ever lived. We don't have to do any of the cooking (or any of the cleaning up afterward). All we have to do is show up at the party and enjoy the meal.[9]

That doesn't mean we don't have to work at a job to support ourselves and our families. And it doesn't mean our work won't be difficult and frustrating. Futility and toil are aspects of the Fall that we men simply have to face.

> "Cursed is the ground because of you; through painful toil you will eat of it all the days of your life. It will produce thorns and thistles for you, and you will eat the plants of the field. By the sweat of your brow you will eat your food until you return to the ground, since from it you were taken; for dust you are and to dust you will return."[10]

The last sentence says it all. "You will have to work your tail off just to eat until you die." Some key phrases stand out in this passage, such as "painful toil," "all the days of your life," "sweat of your brow," and "until you return to the ground." We have a catchphrase that sums it up: "There's no rest for the weary."

Authentic manhood requires that we come to terms with the truth that one of the ramifications of work is that it seems pointless and wears us out. As a way of teaching us dependence, God has made work futile, toilsome, and empty. We are not meant to depend on our own efforts to get by. The curses doled out in Genesis 3 are opportunities for us to depend on God and not on our own strength.

The Villages

My (David's) dad recently retired after forty-three years as an educator. I wrote him a long letter for his retirement party, acknowledging his accomplishments and what I had learned from watching him vocationally over my lifetime. I spoke of having encountered dozens of my father's employees and colleagues over the years and how they would speak of his integrity and his leadership. My dad's celebration was a time of honoring a great man and the contributions he had made to the field of education.

If the truth be told, however, I've had a hard time truly celebrating his retirement, because I'm just so darn jealous. I call him sometimes around 10:00 a.m. these days, and he's still reading the newspaper, on his third cup of coffee, and hanging out in his robe. Or he calls me from the road. He and my mom are traveling like two people who've never been outside the city limits. He called me the other morning from California—they had been exploring the wine country. They are also busy planning a trip to Europe. And I know that's exactly how it should be. My dad began working to make money early in his adolescence. He worked his way through college and had three jobs when I was born. And he worked every day since, until his well-earned retirement.

His first job out of undergrad was teaching accounting at a rural high school while attending graduate school at night. He married my mom soon after, and I arrived on the scene about a year and a half into their marriage. My mom was eighteen when she and my dad married. She was twenty when I was born. So, here was my dad in his early twenties, married, about to become a father for the very first time, teaching during the day, going to graduate school at night, and working various odd jobs to make ends meet and provide for his family. He worked as a desk manager at a hotel on the weekends, led the choir and youth group on Wednesdays and Sundays at their church, held a job as a teller at a bank in the summers, and a handful of other odd jobs pieced together to pay the bills. It was important to both my parents that my mother be a stay-at-home mom in the early years of our lives. My mom was committed to pouring everything she had into us. I've heard my parents tell dozens of stories about this season in their marriage; and with the sacrifices they had to make, I don't know how they managed to do it.

My dad supported a family of four for decades, put two children through college, gave both of his kids amazing weddings, and helped them buy their first homes. It's about time for the guy to kick up his feet and read the paper all morning. So why am I begrudging him this well-deserved season of rest? The truth is that I'm jealous of most all retired people. Retired people who do retirement well, that is.

I also happen to know the queen of retirement. Her name is Jacqueline Baker, and she's my wife's grandmother. We all call her Miss Jackie. My kids call her Grandmother, pronouncing it like "grondmother," with a strong emphasis on the "grand."

Miss Jackie is adorable. She is about five feet tall when she doesn't have her high heels on (which is only when she's in the tub, I'm told), with short blonde hair and radiant features. She is always dressed to kill. She wears a fitted suit, like Jackie O, during the day and silk pajamas and robes at night. (Her bedroom slippers even have heels and are either studded or feathered.) She drives a long, white Cadillac with a tan leather interior, although we have strong concerns about how well she can see over the dashboard. She is eighty-five years old, completely elegant, and also feisty. (I like that in a retiree, a little fire in the belly.)

She lives in Lady Lake, Florida, in a retirement community called The Villages. Here's what their Web page boasts:

> Remember enjoying good times while
> on vacation with family and friends?
> The excitement of what to do each
> day and the possibilities of tomorrow
> and wishing that it didn't have to end?
>
> Retirement life at The Villages in
> Florida is like being on a permanent
> vacation! Here you'll discover the per-
> fect place to enjoy life as you've always
> dreamed.
>
> In the heart of every great retire-
> ment community there's a special
> place "where good friends gather for a
> great time."[11]

Bring on the permanent vacation!

I've asked Miss Jackie to claim the place next door for me. I love the setup at this place. It's all these ador-able little folks driving around in fancy golf carts (they decorate them for Christmas), traveling from water aerobics to shuffleboard, archery to scuba diving, billiards to water volleyball, salsa dancing to yoga. I love it. They have more activities, more restaurants, more swimming pools, and more sunshine in a ten-mile radius than you could find anywhere else on the planet.

Miss Jackie has a dog named Dixie, a small dachshund, who is just as feisty and stylish as her owner. If Dixie could wear heels, I swear she would. Instead, she wears floral and rhinestone collars. And you should see her perched on the front seat of the golf cart or in Miss Jackie's Caddie. They are quite a pair.

Dixie's a barker, and that's been a bit of an issue with one of her neighbors. When the only thing you've got to get worked up over is the limited supply of mangoes at Publix or the rising cost of pharmaceuticals, Dixie is an easy target. Miss Jackie has resolved the barking issues by rewarding Dixie with an abundance of treats if she darts out in the yard, takes a quick poop, and darts back in without making a racket. Who wouldn't work with that arrangement?

Well, I'd like to have Miss Jackie's setup. Or at least Dixie's. I was made for retirement. I was created for golf carts, shuffleboard, salsa dancing, sunshine, and hours with the *New York Times*. I'll get me a Dixie, and we'll wear matching polos in the spring and summer.

Something's Gotta Give

Rodney Rothman wrote a memoir, called *Early Bird*, about retiring in his thirties. He settled in to one of those retirement communities in Florida, much like The Villages. I studied the book, hoping to find suggestions on how to get there in my thirties, but I've yet to find a way.

Why am I so infatuated with the idea of retirement?

For me, the hook involves giving up what I imagine to be a lifelong battle. What my dad didn't teach me (or maybe he did and I just couldn't wrap my mind around it until now) was that I would spend the bulk of my adult life being worn out and lonely and out of balance, just so I can bring home the bacon.

I don't ever remember my dad teaching me that being a man would involve this much sacrifice and compromise and exhaustion. And even if he had, I don't think I could have believed his words until I was living in the middle of that reality.

As a young father, I think I lived under the illusion that I could be both fully present as a husband and father and fully present as a therapist and writer. But something's gotta give. And at the end of the day, what gives is too often me.

Three kids later, I have an even greater respect for my father and the commitment he made to me, my sister, and our mother. Balancing a full-time job, writing, teaching, and family is an ongoing struggle for me—one that I am usually failing at miserably. And I'm darn tired, for a man in his thirties.

Sure, I make decent sacrifices on both sides that afford opportunities for me to be a better therapist or a better father or a better husband. Sometimes, I balance all this well, but most times I don't. Some days, I tend far better to other people's relationships than I do my own. Some days, I listen with more focus and curiosity to other people's children than I do my own. Some days, I challenge men to love their wives in ways that my own wife can only dream of experiencing. And then some days I love my family well. But all this fighting for balance can wear a man out!

What I do know now is that I will continue to live with this tension for years to come. To provide well for my family means I have to keep working. The illusion I'm living with right now is that the majority of things I'm sacrificing now will be made right in retirement. And I'm not trading in that dream until my mid-sixties. So bring on the permanent vacation!

I am beginning to see that, for me, this infatuation

with retirement speaks to a much fuller longing I have for rest.

Labor always costs us something. Even if we get paid the big bucks (not that I do), work takes from us our time, energy, and attention. Time spent at work (even if we love it) is time spent away from other things we love, like family, friends, hobbies, passions, and so on. Especially if we enjoy what we do, we can wear ourselves out doing it.

Rest for the Weary

The balance that many of us men are fighting for is between work and home. But really that's off the mark. The balance we need to be after is the balance between work and rest. Too many men work more outside the home than they work for the holiness of their families. The more responsibility we have (job, marriage, kids, family, friends, church), the more room we need in our lives for recreation, regeneration, and rejuvenation.

The creation story in Genesis depicts for us how hard God worked. He hovered, created, spoke, made, and finished. He was busy getting the job done. And then he did something else. He rested. Rest provided God the space and perspective to experience pleasure with what he made. That is the thing I (David) observe with my dad right now. I have never seen him delight so much in life. Sadly, like my dad did in his thirties, I'm missing many opportunities to delight in my present life. I hope that I can begin to find in my life today a measure of what my dad knows. As he moves more deeply into rest, it exposes my need for rest too.

Exhausting ourselves through our vocations and callings, which leaves us with little left for the other significant parts of our lives, is at its core a very crafty form of idolatry. Labor must come out of our abundance. When it does not, we worship the work of our own hands and the effort of our own willpower.

How we labor and how we rest always expose the truth about our internal relationship with God, others, and ourselves. How well we understand the art of work and rest in our lives, and live out that understanding on a daily basis, speaks to how well we mirror God's image as men. In many ways, the art of work and rest is the physical expression of our internal reality and our relationship with God.

Interestingly, there is not a commandment to work in the Ten Commandments, but there is one for us to rest. The Bible acknowledges that uninterrupted work makes for demoralized toil. You see, in Scripture the work ethic is derived from a "rest ethic" mandated in the Sabbath. We are called to rest and made to work.

The biblical idea of rest has more to do with trusting

in God for the daily doings than it does the concept of putting our feet up and taking it easy. Some of the hardest work we will ever do is learning to rest in God's care. But it's in returning to this place (with God) in rest, quietness, and trust that we find a safe enough place to close our eyes and slow down for a while.

Back and Forth

The Bible seems to say a lot about working and resting. One book, Ecclesiastes, directly addresses the tension between work and rest (and the blessing of both). In the canon of Scripture, Ecclesiastes is a pretty strange book. As the author contends, "Everything is meaningless."[12] It sounds kind of bleak, don't you think? On the surface, the message of the book seems simple: "You work and then you die. So fear God." But upon closer examination, there is a lot of hope to be found. The book asks a very profound question. At the end of the day, it is not a question of whether you will work or rest, but rather, why do you work and why do you rest—for yourself or for God?

That's a pretty good question in our day and age, when the clash between work and leisure is at an all-time high. Are we living (working and resting) to secure our own power and happiness? Or are we living (working and resting) in response to who God is and who

HOW TO NEGOTIATE A RAISE

Very few people actually ask for a raise, so if you want one, you gotta ask for it. Your organization will assume you're satisfied unless you ask for a pay raise.

1. **THE ASK.** Approach your boss and say, "I'm interested in a pay raise. How responsive do you feel our organization would be to an adjustment in my compensation?" Asking the question in this way does a few things. It allows you to approach the subject in a friendly manner with your supervisor. This question also gives you the opportunity to let the company know you are evaluating this issue. It also doesn't pit you against your boss but focuses the decision on the company. Then ask when it would be convenient to talk about this further. The goal is for both sides to set a specific time to discuss a pay raise.

2. **THE ATTITUDE.** Short of blackmail, it's really difficult to force your boss to give you a raise. And let's face it, blackmail will either get you fired, put in jail, or at best damage your working relationship. So as you approach your boss and the meeting, stay open-minded and positive. Remember to keep a helpful and constructive attitude throughout the process, and let your supervisor know that you appreciate the time that he or she has taken to consider this issue on your behalf. (You need to understand that many supervisors want to give you a pay raise, but they are often constrained by other conditions.) You want

your boss to know that you will listen and try to understand his or her views. Avoid ultimatums or threats.

3. **THE PREP.** Negotiating a raise can be uncomfortable for many people (both you and your boss). First, have an idea of your fair-market value. There are numerous ways to inform yourself about this. (Check with your professional organization, contact a job recruiter, look at other, similar job listings, surf monster.com, etc.) This process will keep your expectations realistic and fair.

Next, you need to keep track of your accomplishments for your organization and be ready to present your list of accomplishments to your boss. Be prepared to discuss your accomplishments and your overall value by thinking of answers to the following questions:

What value are you delivering to your organization?

Can you list your accomplishments over the past year?

How have these accomplishments benefited the organization?

These questions will assist you in negotiating your raise within the organization. You also need to enter your negotiation certain that you are delivering what your organization expects. You must not only meet your organization's expectations, but also focus on exceeding these expectations in order to motivate them to give you a raise.

Finally, consider your boss's needs. Like you, your boss has requirements. To persuade him or her to say yes, your ideas will have to address the things that are important to your supervisor and your company.

4. **THE MEETING.** When it comes time for the meeting, have a written document that includes the following things:

> Highlight your recent and historical accomplishments with the firm. It is far easier to persuade someone to agree with your proposal if he or she sees how that proposal is firmly grounded on objective criteria, such as what similar firms pay people with your experience or what others in the company make.

> Provide multiple options for your desired compensation. Create possible solutions to present to your boss, and then work through them together. Offer other ways that you are willing to be compensated (extra vacation days, a more flexible schedule, stock options, a bonus, profit sharing, funds for additional training).

> Don't lowball yourself. Psychological research shows that the more you ask for, the more you will get in negotiation. At the same time, be realistic. Only offer ideas to which your boss can logically say yes.

Have a plan B. Unless your boss says yes, you need to have a backup plan. Part of your preparation should be the creation of a specific action plan so you know what you'll do if you have to walk away from the table.

Adapted from Roberta Chinsky Matuson, "Think You Deserve a Raise? Ask for It," http://career-advice.monster.com/salary-negotiation/human-resources/management/ Think-You-Deserve-a-Raise-Ask-for-I/home.aspx; and Therese Droste, "Ask for the Raise You Want," http://career-advice.monster.com/salary-negotiation/Ask-for-the-Raise-You-Want/ home.aspx; and Marshall Loeb, "What You Shouldn't Do When Asking for a Raise," www.collegejournal.com/successwork/onjob/20070904-loeb.html.

he made us to be? Too often, we get trapped in the cycle of "stuff" (cars, houses, boats, LCD TVs, financial security, etc.), and we have what Ecclesiastes calls a "rest-less" existence. You see, if we are working for control and happiness, then we will have little room for relationship, because we will see everybody else as a competitor. People become either objects of envy or obstacles to overcome in our pursuit of our goals.

Ecclesiastes proposes a perplexing paradox: Work is essential to finding fulfillment, but work alone is meaningless and vain. Recreation and celebration are equally important, and yet too much of it will numb us, dull us, and destroy us. The issue is one that cuts to the very heart of human worth and purpose—a question that men wrestle with every day. If life is all about work, it is bankrupt. If life is all about rest, it is pointless. So, what are we to do?

If we don't find deeply satisfying meaning in our labor, life is empty. If our work is mostly about attempting to manufacture our own security, we will expend years of energy in an effort to gain a modicum of power and safety. We will commit ourselves to production and keep score by counting our profits. To keep us satisfied, this lifestyle requires constant attention and effort.

But the opposite extreme is equally dangerous. If we

don't find cause for celebration in our rest, we are boring. We live self-centered lives based on the consumption of people and things.

What a bind! Ecclesiastes ultimately offers a way out of the cycle of futility. There is one pleasure of human activity that provides meaning and, ultimately, enjoyment: vocation. Not vacation . . . vocation.

The idea of vocation is more akin to a *calling* than to mere labor. It's doing a kind of work that is expressive of your unique heart and marking by God. Ecclesiastes says that to find this kind of work is the ultimate gift, which comes only from God. If you like what you do, then it doesn't matter whether it amounts to a hill of beans; you will live passionately. When you are pursuing a true calling, you will be willing to go through great pain in order to get to do what you desire.

Life is far too painful not to spend your days fully alive in what you do (in both work and rest). Every man will be restless until he wrestles enough with his story and with God to discover the things that make him come alive. As we practice the art of work and rest (calling and surrender), we will receive more than we can ever ask or imagine. We will discover who we are made to be and what we are made to do.

Lessons Learned

1. Work = sacrifice + loss.

2. Worship = everything we do for the glory of God.

3. Balance = work + rest.

4. Balance = work + family.

5. Heaven, apparently, is in Lady Lake, Florida.

How to Move On from Here

Ask yourself a couple of questions: How does my work reflect God's creativity, mercy, justice, service, sacrifice, and love? How is my labor more about personal gain, acclaim, recognition, or security? Give yourself several sentences or a few paragraphs to expand on these questions. In doing this exercise, you will gain some insight into how work defines your worldview.

Consider how the following statement affects your perspective of rest: "The biblical idea of rest has more to do with trusting God for the daily doings than it does the concept of putting our feet up and taking it easy." Where are you having trouble trusting God?

Spend some time evaluating whether you are passionate about your work and if you are living out of the center of who God made you to be, in terms of your vocation. If not, we suggest that you consider addressing this area specifically. Most of us will spend more time working than doing anything else in our adult lives. Check out some resources at www.48days.com, read *What Color Is Your Parachute?*, or spend some time with a qualified career counselor.

CHAPTER 6

Pinewood Derby

The Art of Collaboration

The Pinewood Derby is one of the most popular and successful family activities in Cub Scouting. If you didn't know, Pinewood Derby cars are small, wooden race cars that Cub Scouts make with help from their families. (Or, more accurately, they're race cars that parents make with some help from their Cub Scouts.) The cars, powered by gravity, run down a track in a competition that includes the entire Cub Scout pack. The Pinewood Derby is an annual event in most packs, and it is the cause of either great joy or great pain.

The first Pinewood Derby was organized in 1953 in a Cub Scout pack in Manhattan Beach, California. Since then, nearly 100 million kits have been sold. The stated purpose of the Pinewood Derby is to "help the Cub Scout build a team relationship with [his] parent or helper, experience the sense of accomplishment and the excitement of competition, learn Win/Lose good sportsmanship, and to have fun."[1] The hidden agenda is that grown men devote hours of their time in order to build a car that can win the competition and smoke every other dad.

I (Stephen) still have it somewhere—the car my dad and I made. Like any other Pinewood Derby car, she began as a simple block of wood, nails, plastic wheels, and a sheet of instructions. With box in hand, I followed my dad down the steps to the basement, past the hot-water heater, to the darkest corner of the basement, where he kept his workbench.

I was just tall enough that my chin could rest on the surface of the workbench. The underside of my chin pressed into the rough plywood top, and the edge dug into the tender skin of my neck. I was eye level with the pile of parts and pieces. The fluorescent light hanging overhead filled the air with a muted hum and painted everything a pasty white. Raw possibility lay right before my eyes.

As my dad read over the directions, excitement coursed through my veins. I could feel it in my fingers and toes, and even in the tips of my hair. I radiated impatience. Dad handed me some graph paper and asked me to draw out what I wanted the car to look like. I immediately ran to my room and began to dream. What must have been several hours later, I returned with a design for a Formula One/Indy-style race car. Airfoil, big tires, cockpit—the whole thing. My dad gently steered me in a different direction. He taught me about aerodynamics and how in order to make the car go as fast as possible, it needed to have as few edges as possible. He and I negotiated the design until we agreed. In the end, what we came up with looked like a doorstop on wheels—a really fast doorstop on wheels.

Night after night, I waited for him to get home from work so that we could go down into the dark basement to work on my car. Like most Pinewood Derby projects with a dad involved, I was allowed to do a little bit of work (sanding and painting, mostly), but he did the largest part of the job. Most nights, I would have to go to bed while my dad continued cutting, boring, sanding, filing—sculpting really—this block of wood into a perfectly balanced racing machine that would carry the hopes and dreams of a second-grade boy (and his father, if the truth be told).

I named my car The Falcon. She was painted a metallic emerald green and was shellacked to a glossy finish. She had two white pinstripes that ran down the top of the car from tail to tip. The letters F-A-L-C-O-N ran parallel to the stripes. She was beautiful. And she was fast.

On the night of the big competition, we walked into

my elementary school cafeteria and found the room buzzing with energy. All the lunch tables had been folded and pushed against the walls. At the front of the cafeteria, next to the stage, was the track—four lanes wide and sloped like the upper half of a ski jump.

There were people everywhere. Mothers and fathers milled about, drinking stale coffee and talking, while small groups of boys in their pressed navy scout uniforms darted and weaved in and out of the adults like schools of fish through a coral reef.

Upon arrival, each boy had to take his car to be checked in. There it was weighed, measured, and inspected to see if it met all of the qualifications and specifications. Once deemed legal for competition, each car was assigned a heat in which it would race. The top two cars from each heat would move to the next bracket until there were only four cars left.

When my heat was called, my father nudged me forward, and I handed my car over to the scoutmaster, who was placing the cars on the track. The murmuring of conversation died down, and the scoutmaster said, "On your marks! Get set! Go!" With that, he pulled the handle that released the cars down the track. I held my breath until the official result was announced.

In my first heat, The Falcon won. In fact, heat after heat, The Falcon won. At first I was shocked; but as the heats progressed, I grew more confident. My doorstop on wheels was proving to be a race car on fire.

By the end of the night, I found myself in the championship race. I watched with anticipation as the four finalists were lined up across the track. Again, the familiar cadence of the scoutmaster's voice rose above the noise of the boys and their parents: "On your marks! Get set! Go!"

Amid a cacophony of voices, the final four rattled down the track. When the results were announced, I had finished third. A bit disappointing, but not all that bad.

The scoutmaster quieted the crowd again, and after giving a short speech thanking everybody and espousing the values of competition, working together, and things like that, he called out the names of the award winners. When he called out my name, I walked up and got my ribbon. Even though I finished third, I felt as if I had won a gold medal. Standing up in front of the whole pack to receive my ribbon and the recognition of my peers was a powerful experience. It was the first time I had ever succeeded at anything resembling formal competition. I loved how that felt. I wanted more of it. A few weeks later, we attended the district Pinewood Derby. There, I was put out in the first race, finishing fourth in my heat.

HOW TO WIN THE PINEWOOD DERBY

The first thing you need to know is that the Pinewood Derby is not about the actual race at all. It's about dads and sons. It's about time spent together and memories made.

At least that's how it was designed.

However, just as grown men have turned Saturdays at the Pop Warner football field into the Super Bowl, the Pinewood Derby has evolved into a secondary competition between dads. There are entire books, pamphlets, and online resources devoted to the secrets to winning the coveted Pinewood Derby, and you can bet they weren't written by a fourth-grade Cub Scout. And when you walk through the door on race day, there will be no question as to whose dad is the mechanical engineer and whose dad is a therapist.

So before you begin, determine what kind of dad you want to be. Do you want the Pinewood Derby to be a father/son bonding experience, in which you and your lad contribute equally to the researching, designing, and building of the car? Or do you want to be the guy who is so determined to win the race that he'll risk ruining the experience with his son in the name of victory?

While you're deciding which guy you are, here are a couple of things to keep in mind:

1. **UNLESS YOU'RE A MASTER WOODWORKER** or a mechanical engineer, you're not going to win the awards for best design or fastest car.

2. **THE MOST SIGNIFICANT LESSONS IN LIFE** are learned through losing, not winning. The Pinewood Derby can

teach some significant life lessons, such as collaboration, humility, communication, planning, compromise, and attention to detail, just to name a few. Focus on building your relationship with your son, and you'll reap the greater rewards of the experience.

When you and your son are ready to start building your car, here are some helpful hints:

1. **RESEARCH AND PLANNING.** Search "How to win the Pinewood Derby" on Google. You'll find more than 80,000 hits that will give you some directions. We suggest Randy Worcester's Ultimate Pinewood Derby Site (http://members.aol.com/randywoo/pine/). When building a Pinewood Derby, good planning is essential.

2. **DESIGN.** Keep it simple. Start with a wedge shape. This basic design is easy to sand and has plenty of wood in the back for the weights. Have your son draw a design (top and side view) on graph paper, then cut it out and use it as a template. (Avoid making the front of the car pointed. It's difficult to set up against the starting dowels on the racetrack.)

3. **PIECES AND PARTS.** The most important part of the car is not the wood. It's the weight, wheels, axles, and lubricants.

4. **WEIGHT.** Get the weight as close to the five-ounce limit as possible. Keep the weight to the back of the car, so that gravity can act on the weight for a longer period of time during the race. (But be careful not to put too much

weight in the rear or you'll pop a wheelie!) Keep the weight low on the car and balanced in the center (left-to-right) of the car. Remember, the official scale may not weigh the same as yours at home. So, bring some lead tape from the golf shop with you to the event.

5. **WHEELS.** Get rid of all of the ridges and edges on the wheels—inside and out—with 600-grit-or-finer sandpaper. (Don't sand too much or you'll create a flat spot.) Have only three wheels touching the track. (This will decrease friction.) Wax the wheels with solvent-free furniture polish.

6. **AXLES.** Polish the axles three times. First with 400-grit sandpaper, then 600-grit, and finally a jeweler's rouge. Finish off with a chrome/metal polish. Axles must be straight front to back (square to the body). Glue the axles in place. Nothing is worse than having a wheel fall off as you cross the finish line.

7. **LUBRICATION.** Friction is your enemy. Graphite, the lubricant of choice, has a low friction coefficient (which is what you want).

Adapted from Randy Worcester's Ultimate Pinewood Derby Site: http://members.aol.com/randy-woo/pine.

I learned something really important that day: I hated losing more than I enjoyed winning.

Camping with the Critters

When I (David) was a boy, I, too, had a brief stint in the Scouts. It started in the late 1970s and ended in the late 1970s. I hate to admit it, because I am such an advocate of scouting. I really love the organization. There are so few institutions in our culture that offer boys that kind of opportunity for risk, adventure, and building life skills, all in the context of male community. Male initiation is a lost art, for the most part, with the exception of the rituals still being provided in the world of the Boy Scouts of America.

I know several young men who are Eagle Scouts. I've attended some of their ceremonies and watched as they were bestowed this honor. I'm secretly hoping that someday I'll have championed the scouting organization long enough and made enough significant contributions to the development of boys that they'll give me an honorary Eagle award, the way Oprah got an honorary PhD, even though she didn't do the work. But it hasn't happened yet, so I'm doing my own scouting experiences with my sons until *they* are old enough to join officially. And as is the case with most things for me, I'm flying by the seat of my pants—navigating without a compass.

We didn't camp as a family when I was growing up. My dad wasn't a Scout. And my mother and sister aren't the outdoors type. They don't do bugs or heat or tents or state-park showers. However, my mom was the den mother for a year of my Cub Scout experience, which says a lot about how she sacrificed on my behalf. You'd have to meet my mom to really understand what I'm talking about. She is a picture of Southern hospitality, ripped off the pages of a Jan Karon novel. My mother is beautiful, poised, gracious, always looks like a million bucks, and keeps a home like a Martha Stewart apprentice. She's not exactly the den mother type, but she ponied up while all the other mothers were hiding in the back of the room praying, "Don't pick me!"

Mom was still working within her giftings when we attempted the cooking badge, but the knot tying and survival skills sent her too deep into unfamiliar territory. I also had a tendency to be a bit of a firework when it came to extracurricular stuff. I had great passion and interest in the beginning—went off with a bang but fizzled out at some point soon after. The combination of that and my mother's disinterest in learning to dig a latrine brought the scouting experience to an early halt.

So, I'm working with limited survival skills as I enter the world of camping with my own boys. My good buddy Trace has a son who was born within a day of my boys, and they love spending time together. Trace has about as much experience as I do, so we are quite a pair. The other thing we share in common is that we didn't start having kids in our twenties. That means that when our kids hit adolescence, we'll be pushing fifty and will be extremely limited in the things we can do. We just can't keep up with the young dads, those guys who married right out of college and started working on a family within a year or two. Take my parents, for example. My mom was eighteen when she married my dad. She had me when she was twenty. When I was old enough to drive a car, she was only thirty-six. I, on the other hand, will be applying for Social Security when my kids are going to college. My parents are these really fun, active, healthy, "get down on the floor and wrestle" kind of grandparents. If my children wait until their mid-thirties to have kids, I may never even meet the grandkids. And if I do, I won't likely have hearing or eyesight. I'll be old and crusty, and they will just pet me like an aged beagle, while saying things like, "You look good, Granddaddy" and "We brought you more of that peanut brittle you like so much. PEANUT BRITTLE, GRANDDADDY!

THE KIND YOU LIKE. . . . WE PUT IT NEXT TO YOUR OXYGEN TANK." I'll smile, and then they'll straighten the afghan I have in my lap and pet me again.

Being an older dad makes camping much more difficult. The biggest issue is the sleep. In my twenties, I could sleep anywhere, anytime, and for as long as I wanted. I can't do that anymore. I need to be in my own bed with a down pillow, and I have a lot of props to assist my sleep—a sound machine, a fan that blows directly on me, and medicine for insomnia. So what's a guy with a bunch of sleep props to do on a campout? Trace and I wrestled with this for a while and decided we'd do our first campout at his house. We'd start when the boys turned four. We'd pitch a tent on his bonus-room floor but still do the whole camping deal. We roasted hot dogs and marshmallows in his backyard (we just used his gas grill instead of an open fire); we had flashlights, sleeping bags, and all the gear. We just did it *indoors* the first time out. We called it Urban Professional Older Dad Camping. It worked well the first time. Really well, actually. The boys slept in the tent, and I set up all my sleep props in Trace's guest bedroom.

We agreed the next morning that the official first campout was a huge success and we could consider

graduating to the outdoors next time around. Then my
wife heard about a local deal sponsored by the Nashville Zoo, called Camping with the Critters. The *idea*
of it sounded great. You come and throw your tent on
the zoo property, they provide the campfire and all the
food, you bring *your* critters, and then you get to wander around the zoo and look at *their* critters. You get a
late-night zoo walk with your flashlights to see what the
elephants do in the dark. *My* critters could hardly con-
tain themselves when I introduced the idea to them.

I called Trace, and we agreed we could pull it off.
We made a reservation, decided on a time to meet after
work on Friday, and showed up with all our gear in tow.
We arrived to discover that everyone else present was a
card-carrying, seasoned, zoo-camping parent. They had
all descended on the grounds hours before we arrived,
had staked out their campsites, pitched their tents in
strategic locations, and were already engaged in the fun.
We dropped off our gear near some other tents and
immediately jumped into the planned activities. An
hour into the fun, we realized it would soon be dark, so
we wrapped things up at one of the exhibits and headed
back to our campsite (also known as the only place left
to pitch a tent, because all the good spots were taken).
We began pitching our tents (our fancy REI tents that
we had assembled on only one other occasion). There

were so many parts and poles, canopies and nets. How did they fit it all in that bag? I'd still like to know.

I'm convinced that assembling a tent as nighttime descends would be a great challenge to any man. But to a therapist and an attorney who had, like, sixteen months of combined camping experience dating back to the 1970s, this was an even greater challenge. At one point, I looked over and made eye contact with the big guy at the campsite next door, who was sipping a Mountain Dew and chuckling. He had turned his pop-up chair to face the two of us, and we were obviously providing him with some good entertainment. Periodically, I heard him chuckle and wheeze. A couple of times it evolved into an asthmatic, choking kind of laughing. His taunting was both irritating and motivating.

When he spoke, he said things like, "This the first time you guys have camped?"

I hollered back, "First time at the zoo, but not the first time camping." I glared at Trace with a look that said, *Don't you dare tell him that the only other time we've done this was in your den.*

We kept sliding poles together, poking them through the slips, hoping it was the right opening, because neither one of us could see the darn instructions. My tent would rise and collapse, rise and collapse. Mountain

Dew chuckled louder. I sensed we might have been better than Comedy Central for the guy. At one point, he left to find his wife. I imagine he hunted her down at the campfire to say, "Honey, you've gotta come watch these two goobers pitching tents in the dark." Moments later, he threw her a chair and got her a beverage.

Meanwhile, our boys, Baker, Witt, and Davis, were milling around, wearing their little miner-type helmets with flashlights attached. We asked them to shine their headlights toward the instructions, but it was useless. Try telling a four-year-old boy to hold still and shine the light in one location. We finally just gave up on their assistance. They just kept moving their heads around and asking, "Why is it taking so long?"

The dad at the site next to us eventually offered to help. I think what was entertainment for him was painful to watch for his wife. She must've taken pity on us and told Mountain Dew to get up and make himself useful. At this point, Trace didn't wait for my stubborn, competitive, Type A, firstborn inclination to resist the offer and immediately said, "Absolutely." So Mountain Dew popped up and brought his expertise to the situation. By now it was pitch black. I'm certain some families were turning in for bed. Half the animals at the zoo were two hours into a good night's sleep.

Half an hour later, we had two tents assembled (the guy didn't even need the instructions), began roasting some dogs for our starving sons, and then settled in for the night. I could hear the gibbons calling to one another in the background and thought to myself, *If those monkeys scream all night long, I'm gonna lose it.* I tried to ignore the noise, took my sleep medicine, tucked the boys in their sleeping bags, and then slid into mine.

It was a brand-new bag. I had purchased it the same day I bought the REI tent, but I'd never been in it. (Remember, I slept in the guest bedroom on the previous campout.) The young fella who sold me the bag looked to be around twenty-one or twenty-two, maybe in his last year at Vanderbilt. He went on and on about the mummy bag and its popularity—how I would stay warm, even in below freezing temperatures. I was sold.

It didn't occur to me that I would only be camping in the spring and fall in Tennessee, where the temps aren't likely to dip below the fifties. So there I lay, burning up and unable to spread my legs apart. The mummy bag provides an experience akin to a sack race at a picnic—a person bound up trying to accomplish a nearly impossible task. I couldn't move about, and I'm a stretcher, a twister, and a turner when it comes to sleep.

I also needed my fan and my sound machine. I had brought my down pillow, but it kept sliding out of the mummy bag. I kept having to slither after it. And, of course, we were on a slope (because all the good campsites on flat ground had been taken by the time we arrived). The monkeys were calling, and then one of my boys started snoring. He has all kinds of allergies, so he was stopped up from something in bloom. I slithered over in the mummy bag to try to shake him. He's a mover, too, and had managed to work his way out of his own bag. I tucked him back in, and then my other son woke up and had to pee.

I unzipped the door and walked him out behind the tent. I looked over at Mountain Dew's setup and could hear his circular fan blowing from outside the tent. I imagined it to be providing adequate air and noise, probably powered by some portable generator. "Jerk," I mumbled.

My son said, "What did you say, Daddy?"

"Nothing, son. Just pee and let's go back inside the tent."

We climbed back in and zipped the door closed, but then my other son woke up with the noise and announced he had to poop. (Who has to poop in the middle of the night? Answer me that.) So we put our shoes on and headed off for the bathrooms. By the time

HOW TO BUILD A FIRE

This is a big deal, guys. Building a great fire brings honor and reverence in the company of other men. (Not to mention how much your wife will appreciate it.) A strong and well-contained fire is the practical centerpiece of outdoor survival. Everybody loves sitting or standing around an open fire on a cold evening.

Before we can talk about how to build it, let's make sure we have everything we need: a secure fire pit, dry wood, kindling (little sticks or pieces of wood that light easily), a starting medium (crumpled newspaper, dry leaves, or dry grass), and a match or lighter. Also, a bucket of water or sand (just in case). Now, let's get this thing started.

1. Make sure all the guys are ready to stand around and watch you do your work. Be prepared for input and suggestions. (Every guy's got an opinion on how to build a fire when he's merely observing.) You won't need any additional input if you keep reading.

2. Build a little "log cabin" or "tepee" with the kindling.

3. Place leaves, grass, or paper inside the cabin or tepee.

4. Have some larger pieces of wood ready to build a larger tepee or cabin around the smaller one once it catches fire.

5. Light the paper, grass, or leaves. Once it catches a little, blow on it. As the little cabin or tepee starts to burn, build a bigger one around it. Be prepared to add some more paper on top of the smaller cabin or tepee. This will enable the fire to start burning a bit quicker.

6. Once the fire is going, keep an eye on it and add more wood as needed, but avoid smothering the fire with wood. Don't bombard the tepee; adding firewood is a slow art.

7. Pay attention to Smokey Bear: Never leave a fire unattended.

8. When you're done with the fire, douse it with water or sand. Make sure it's out before you leave it.

Adapted from Jeffery Lee, *Catch a Fish, Throw a Ball, Fly a Kite: 21 Timeless Skills Every Child Should Know (and Any Parent Can Teach!)* (Random House, 2004); and "How to Build a Campfire in 6 Steps," http://sdsd.essortment.com/howtobuildac_rurd.htm.

we returned, I was even more awake than I had been before. I got the boys settled and broke out my laptop. (Yes, I brought my laptop on the camping adventure. I'm an Urban Professional Older Dad Camper, remember?) I had been watching season five of *24*, and Kiefer Sutherland was my backup plan in case this very thing happened. So there I lay, all strapped, packed, and restricted in the mummy bag, roasting at seventy degrees, listening to the gibbons and Mountain Dew's circular fan, and watching *24*. I got through the remainder of season five that night.

The next morning, Trace fell out of his tent, and we just laughed when we saw each other. Our sons were well rested and ready to go see the reptiles. At breakfast, I shared tales of my night with Kiefer, and Trace spoke of needing to see a chiropractor after sleeping on the ground. We plotted hiring some college guys from our church to take the boys on the next campout.

Now, it's important to note that since that experience a couple of years ago, I've given it another go. I did some hard-core camping with a buddy and his three sons a couple of months ago. By hard-core, I mean in the woods, cooked everything over an open fire, with only a handful of my props. I'm learning to sleep in my mummy bag for two or three hours at a time. Kiefer sat this one out, and apart from a busted lip and needing to see someone about my back this time around, I did well on this adventure. I busted my lip when disassembling the tent. I went to release one of the poles from its tab, and it snapped back and popped me in the mouth. (I told my wife and coworkers that I was wrestling with the boys.)

I'm getting better at it. And I'm committed to doing this with my boys. They love it. They absolutely love the outdoors. No one has made plans to give me an honorary Eagle award, so I'm left to camp without the qualifications. I've decided that's part of my deal. I'm underqualified for the majority of what I do in life. I just keep busting my lip and praying for success.

Periodically, I still have to get the joker at the campsite next to mine to help me pitch the tent—either because it's dark and I can't find my way, or I've lost the instructions, or I never had them in the first place. It's humbling, sometimes humiliating. I want to appear competent in the eyes of my sons, but it's inevitable that they'll see my incompetence. Thankfully, I started camping when they were four. By the time they have memories of our doing it together, they'll think I have some kind of clue. The only record of anything different will be the pages of this book.

Competition vs. Collaboration

I'd also like my sons to witness something unique when they see me interact with the men in my life. Most boys I know don't have a healthy picture of men in relationship. One of three things usually happens.

First, men simply don't do relationships well together. They *exist* in one another's company, but they don't do much more than just that. They might work in the next office over, live in the house down the street, play pickup basketball together on their lunch hour, or even attend the same men's Bible study, but they don't share life together, they don't talk about much more than sports and work, finances and politics. Things stay pretty much on the surface. Instead of sharing the truth about themselves (their feelings, needs, secrets, hopes, struggles) they exchange monologues. One guy states what he thinks about a particular point. Then the other guy shares what he thinks. At best, male friendships are like eating a fine meal from a school cafeteria tray. All the food tastes good, and the flavors even complement each other, but none of the foods are touching; each serving is in its own little compartment.

Second, if guys ever move past coexisting, they usually attempt something that looks closer to authentic relationship, but without any real authenticity. This is especially true among men who know God. There are hundreds of men across the country right now engaged in some kind of Bible study together, who are privately struggling with all kinds of things, unknown to anyone. These guys even participate in "accountability groups" and try to "get real" together, but it becomes mechanical or plastic. It's more reporting than relational.

Sadly, many Christian men seem to think that "authentic relationship" means talking about pornography and lust. They live with the mistaken notion that if they talk about how guys fantasize, lust, and masturbate, then they have gone somewhere *real*.

They relieve each others' shame (somewhat) through confession, but they don't feed each others' hearts with true connection. They may go down the accountability checklist (always culminating in the classic "Have you lied about any of your other answers?"), but they don't really ask each other genuine questions. They aren't curious about who the other guy is, what he thinks, and how he feels. They don't work to draw out the glory of the other man. This is the vegetable soup equivalent of relationship. It may taste good together, but it's not really incorporated and coalesced.

Although this type of interaction is a great beginning and has components of authenticity, it's really more like exhibitionism and voyeurism than authentic relationship. Far too often, guys settle for this kind of relationship. Don't get us wrong—anything that gets guys talking to each other can be good, but there is so much more available to us.

The third thing men do as a substitute for authentic relationship is compete. It's what I (David) was doing with old Mountain Dew at the Nashville Zoo campsite. I was bound and determined not to need this guy's help. Heck, on some level I was competing with Trace to get my tent up before his. How crazy is that? I can't read the directions in the dark, yet I'm still resisting help and trying to beat out my buddy. It's nuts.

Competition starts early in the life of men. Pretty early in our development, we became consumed with our ranking in the pecking order. We began competing in all arenas of life. We raced to see who ran the fastest, who could get the best seat in the car, and who could score the most touchdowns. The list was endless. And this pattern, if not directed well, becomes a means of relating.

The more a man finds his significance in wins and losses, the less able he is to have intimate, authentic, life-giving relationships. Not until we are able to discover our worth in something bigger than ourselves are we able to join with others and bring our whole selves and passions to bear in our relationships.

Many relationships evolve out of a pattern of competing in some way. And this looks dangerous among adult men. Have you ever met a woman who said something like, "It was as if once he 'won me,' he wasn't interested anymore"? Competition can spill over into all aspects of life. We've even seen dads who have trouble not crushing their sons when they coach them, because of their own patterns of finding their significance in winning. (These guys make lousy coaches and even worse spectators.) Sit outside a Little League field anywhere across America and listen to some of the sports-crazed dads ranting and screaming through the chain-link fence, out of their sense of competitiveness.

Most boys don't grow up seeing their dads in healthy, intimate relationships with other men. They don't have a picture of what true male intimacy and relationship look like. They have a very accurate picture of what competition looks like, but not collaboration. When men choose to engage in relationship with one another—genuine, authentic relationship—it can be transformational.

Chicken, Ashamed, or Just Plain Stupid

A lot of men need to mature in their willingness, ability, and capacity for relationship with other men. This is one aspect of life that men frequently screw up. Either because of their woundedness or their shame, they avoid sharing their passions, secrets, and dreams with other men. They fear being seen as less than other men. Sometimes, out of a misguided homophobia, they aren't willing to let their hearts be exposed, enjoyed, and embraced by other men. Whatever the reason, a lot of men are profoundly deficient in their relationships with other guys. We're either chicken, ashamed, or just plain stupid.

Too often, for too many men, when we seek to move into relationship with other guys, it becomes a pissing contest. We try to prove ourselves, instead of giving of ourselves. If we spend our relational energy trying to gain power over another guy (or allow him to pull a power play on us), we squash any potential for authentic relationship. *SPLAT!* Power struggles always kill a relationship. Authentic relationship can only be maintained to the degree that there is fundamental equality between the parties—just as every person has equal value as one of God's image bearers.

If we are able to bypass the destructive forces of one-upmanship, we have the potential for life-giving relationship. The very nature of life proves that we need to partner with others. We can't go it alone. Our need for relationship drives us toward others. We are designed by God for relationship. We are hardwired for it. Our need for it can't be squelched (only numbed for a while).

There's No "I" in Team . . . and There's No "We" Either

Men tend to be hampered in their relationships with other men when they don't understand the distinction between collaboration and teamwork. That's reasonable. Collaboration and teamwork are very similar. But understanding the nuanced differences between the two can help us live more collaboratively in our relationships with other men.

In both collaboration and teamwork, each participant brings his own unique collection of God-given gifts and abilities. These aptitudes run the gamut, from physical gifts to intellectual, emotional, and spiritual gifts. Through our giftedness, we are capable of extraordinary expression and accomplishments. But there's a catch. Our gifts are offset by our limitations and weaknesses. That's why, in spite of our gifts, we need other men. We need to collaborate with guys who can offset our weaknesses.

Collaboration and teamwork are cousins—related, but with some key differences. Both originate in the awareness that I have some gifts and ideas that you don't have, and you have some gifts and ideas that I don't have; and if we are willing to work together, we may be able to accomplish something bigger than ourselves. But how we go about working together will make all the difference. Both collaboration and teamwork are cooperative, but that's where the similarities end.

Collaboration involves humility, meekness, and mutual submission. It's simultaneously recognizing your gifts (dignity) and your limitations (depravity). Teamwork, on the other hand, is more about playing your own position, pulling your own weight, and holding up your end of the bargain.

Collaboration is built around the willingness to give and take for the sake of a shared passion, vision, or purpose. Teamwork is more of an agreement among people to partner together to achieve a common goal.

Collaboration is fluid; teamwork is more structured.

Collaboration is more creative; teamwork is more constructive.

Collaboration is more yielded to the process, whereas teamwork is more directed toward a goal.

Collaboration requires a mutual dependence on each other and on God. Teamwork is also a dependent relationship, but it is more about doing my own job while you do yours, rather than us both putting our hands to the task.

Collaboration is a symphonic harmony. Teamwork is a division of labor.

Collaboration is rooted in the idea that if anyone quits or fails, the whole thing will die and we may never be the same. Teamwork is based on the idea that if a participant is not pulling his weight, he can be replaced with another person who can better serve the interests of the team.

Collaboration is about surrendering our hearts to the trust, care, and encouragement of another person, within a shared vision. Teamwork is more a connection of committed relationships dedicated to leveraging each other's gifts (and covering each other's limitations) in order to obtain the fullest potential of the team.

Collaboration cracks the door to the mysterious work of God's Spirit. Teamwork is focused on cooperative achievement.

Collaboration includes teamwork; but teamwork, though it may include elements of collaboration, does not aspire to the same lofty interdependence.

Killjoys

In our work as counselors with men, we too often see guys try to settle for teamwork when it's collaboration that their hearts truly desire. This is one reason why so many of the Christian men's movements have fallen short. When men come together around a common goal, they often stop at teamwork, even though what their hearts are truly longing for is the intimacy, faith, and camaraderie found in collaboration.

HOW TO USE A SKILL SAW

Not to insult your intelligence, but we're guessing that you may not even know what a skill saw is or what it's used for. So we'll start there. A skill saw (also known as a circular saw) is a hand-held power saw with a circular blade. The blade has different widths and circumferences, which allow precision cutting. The huge advantage of a skill saw is the ability to cut exactly where and how you need to cut: straight lines, angles, and curves. You will never meet a handyman who doesn't own one. It has tremendous value for working with any type of wood-related project. Here are some brief tips:

1. This is dangerous. Be very careful, and don't cut your fingers off. (Think "one-armed man" from *Arrested Development*.)

2. Make sure you are using the correct blade and that it's properly seated and tightened. Always use a sharp blade. Dull blades can bind and overheat. Check the blade guard. Is it in good shape and functioning properly?

3. Set the depth of the blade to no more than one-quarter inch more than the thickness of the wood to be cut. The workpiece is more likely to kick back if you have too much blade exposed.

4. Support the work on both sides. Clamp it on one side if you have to.

5. Look for knots and nails before you begin. Avoid them if possible; if they cannot be avoided, be cautious when approaching them.

6. Start the blade before it meets the wood.

7. Stand to the side when you saw, in case the wood kicks back, and don't overreach.

8. Don't push the saw; just guide it with a little pressure.

9. Let go of the trigger if the blade binds, and stick a wooden shim in the cut to release it.

10. Wait for the blade to completely stop before removing it from the wood.

Warnings:

1. Familiarize yourself with your saw. Read the owner's manual carefully and heed all safety suggestions.

2. Wear goggles and a dust mask when operating your circular saw.

3. Never saw wet wood.

Adapted from Clayton Dekorne, "Choosing and Using a Circular Saw," www.thisoldhouse. com/toh/article/0,,463950,00.html; and Monte Burch, "Tool School: Circular Saws," www. extremehowto.com/xh/article.asp?article_id=60197.

Why do guys stop short when the real deal is within reach? In a word: *pain*.

Every man, somewhere in his heart, has an instinct for collaboration. If you watch little boys play (say, eight years old and younger), they often play collaboratively. They share ideas, are flexible in making up plots, and there's room within their play for varying (and, often, changing) roles within the same activity. Their play is far more creative than that of older boys. There's much less negotiation and much more cooperation. But as boys get older, their play becomes much more competitive, hierarchical, and structured. The older they get, the less collaborative they tend to be. And as things get more competitive, guys start learning how to cover up—how to protect themselves from shame and embarrassment.

Along the way, we've all developed particular styles of relating with others—ways of getting our needs met without being vulnerable. Our own style of relating becomes a way of protecting ourselves. Whether we're outgoing or shy, tough or sensitive, critical or accepting, intellectual or emotional, we've learned how to adapt in order to make our lives work for us. By the time we're adults, our relational styles are a combination of getting our needs met and avoiding the pain of broken promises, damaged relationships, and hard losses. In this context, the structured parameters of teamwork (you do your job and I'll do mine) seem a whole lot safer than the vulnerability of collaboration.

In light of past relational wounds, men stop short of collaboration and try to find contentment in teamwork for three primary reasons: fear of rejection, fear of betrayal, and doubt about God's love.

Whether you've been cut from a team or gotten a poor grade on a test, you know firsthand the sting of coming up short, of not having what it takes. It doesn't take us long to figure out that there are those who *have* and those who *have not*. And when we're the ones who have not, we can end up being used, rejected, or marginalized. It's far less risky to just find our place on the team, do our part, and hope for the best. When we stick our necks out and really invest our hearts and ideas, we set ourselves up to be judged and found wanting.

Even when we give our hearts to a cause in spite of the possibility of not measuring up, there's still the chance that we'll be betrayed by others in whom we've trusted. Every man has experienced being stabbed in the back by someone he trusted. Nothing hurts worse than being deceived, let down, or used by someone we thought was looking out for us.

Even if we are fortunate enough to find and invest in trustworthy relationships where every man tells the truth, gives his heart over to the others, and embraces the process of collaboration, well, we're not out of the woods yet. We still have to come to grips with a God who is beyond our comprehension, a God who may or may not give us the desires of our hearts. Many men have been part of groups that were pursuing noble goals and yet fell short. Part of the mystery of collaboration is that, even when everything else is going right, things can still go wrong.

Rejection, betrayal, and doubt are strong enough forces to keep many guys from stepping beyond the veil of shame and self-protection. They keep secrets about themselves and manage their personal agendas. ("I'll get mine without making myself vulnerable.") Time and again, what begins as the give-and-take of collaboration becomes a tug-of-war for power, protection, or credit, based on past emotional and spiritual wounds. Because of our fear of failure, spiritual abandonment, or relational rejection for not having what it takes, we settle for teamwork (or worse, we begin to compete). We keep score, track individual statistics, and compare results.

As relational beings, we need collaboration if we are going to labor with hope. Collaboration can range from informal associations to formally planned partnerships, but it always provides the environment for relationship building. One important step in collaboration is building a shared vision. A great benefit to collaboration is that it depends and thrives on different perspectives and experiences. But this same diversity is what leads to tension and exposes our desire for power.

In collaborative relationships, communication and time are valued. For any collaborative relationship to occur, trust must be developed and maintained. What makes collaboration so unique is that it is all about the relationship. Production is a by-product of the relational environment. Too often, people will try to establish an open, mutual relationship, but then something happens and they try to force each other to do things.

To build a truly collaborative relationship, it is important that all participants are able to frankly and honestly discuss their own strengths and weaknesses, as well as receive feedback from one another. In order for collaboration to work, every participant must experience that the power is shared (though not necessarily shared equally).

As Benjamin Franklin said at the signing of the Declaration of Independence, "We must all hang together, or assuredly we shall all hang separately."[2] That is the nature of collaboration; if we don't focus on the relationship with each other, we will surely fail (even if we succeed at the planned goal).

Lessons Learned

1. *Winning is fun. Losing is awful.*
2. *There are three ways men tend to avoid authentic relationship.*
3. *Competition kills authentic relationship.*
4. *Collaboration is better than teamwork.*
5. *Men stop short of collaboration.*

How to Move On from Here

What do the guys in your life know about you, really? They might know you are a cigar aficionado or a golf nut or an audiophile. But do they know about the most painful moments in your life—do they know what makes you tick? And do you know that stuff about them? Here is an exercise that might help you see what we are talking about.

Get two sheets of paper. On one sheet make a list of the twenty-five most significant relationships in your life. Friends, family, coworkers, neighbors . . . whoever. Then rate each relationship from a scale of 1–10 (one being the most intimate, ten being the least intimate). You'll probably have no more than one or two people who rank as a one. Now, on another sheet, draw a series of ten concentric circles (like ripples in a pond). On the most inner circles, place whichever names were a one.

And on the second circle place whichever names were a two, and so on.

Looking at your circle diagram, what do you learn from this exercise? Are there any surprises? Who on the list would be surprised by their placement if they saw this? Why? Are they closer to the center or further away than they would expect? Do the people whose names are on the innermost circles know the details of your heart?

What do you need to do to correct any undesirable realities? What aspects of yourself do you need to share with the people on the innermost circles? Who on the outer circles do you want to move closer? Whose help do you need to seek in order to make this happen?

CHAPTER 7

King of the Hill

The Art of Servant Leadership

Over the years in my (David's) counseling practice, I've led several different boys groups. One of the more interesting groups is seventh- and eighth-grade boys. It's a period in a boy's development that is plagued with intense change—physically, emotionally, and relationally. At this stage of adolescence, a young man has five to seven times as much testosterone pouring through his body than at any other age. This hormonal flood causes all kinds of wacky things to happen—random erections, nocturnal emissions, acne, hair growing everywhere, voice changing, mood swings, and so on. It's complete chaos. Some developmental theorists describe this period as one of the worst episodes in a boy's life.

Years ago, I had a kid named Will in my seventh- and eighth-grade group. Will was a kid who fell on the far end of the growth spectrum, meaning he was racing through his physical development. His body could barely keep up with the amount of change that was taking place. He looked like he was two years older than he actually was, and he was built for strength. As he became increasingly aware of his ever-changing body, he began putting himself on display. He went from wearing long-sleeve shirts to three-quarter-length baseball shirts, to tight-fitting, short-sleeve tees, to all muscle shirts. He maintained his personal dress code well into the winter months (when the temperatures dip below freezing in Nashville).

There was no question in my mind about his agenda. He was showcasing his assets. He wanted every guy in the group (and any girl who happened to be in the office, hallway, or parking lot) to see the definition in his arms—the evidence that he was evolving from a gangly adolescent into a muscular man. He began to carry himself differently. He seemed to be fascinated by the physical evolution taking place inside his skin.

One particular Monday, we were wrapping things up with the group and heading out to the parking lot for the parents to retrieve the guys. Will announced that he needed to go to the bathroom. I told him to meet us outside when he was done. The other guys made their way to their respective cars, and when Will's mom pulled up, I informed her that he had made a pit stop. I glanced at my watch, realized I had an appointment, and told her he'd be down within minutes.

On my way to my appointment, I made a swing by the men's room to relieve myself. When I pushed open the door, there stood Will in front of the counter-to-ceiling mirrors—admiring himself. It's important to point out that Will wasn't just looking at himself; he was flexing. He was flexing, posing, and checking out his biceps with admiration and satisfaction—the classic bodybuilder pose. I think he might have kissed those bad boys if I hadn't stepped in when I did.

At the sound of the door, he froze in midpose, looking terrified, busted, and unsure whether to bolt or to make up some outlandish story about checking for ticks or nursing a muscle spasm. He couldn't regain his composure. He just stood there frozen and paralyzed, hoping I would somehow rescue him from the awkwardness.

I thought as quickly as I could about what I had just witnessed and what this kid was hoping to accomplish. Then I gathered my thoughts and said, "Will, my friend, you are a force to be reckoned with!"

Will smiled, froze again, and then ducked his head slightly as he bolted out the door. That kid could not get out of the bathroom fast enough. He left with what I guess was a sense of humiliation and gratitude—obviously embarrassed that I had caught him in the act of admiring and adoring himself, yet absolutely thrilled that I called that kind of attention to him.

It occurred to me that Will wanted the exact same thing we all want as men—someone to acknowledge our strength. Every young man I have ever known wants someone to pay attention to his burgeoning masculinity and to call it out.

I don't think there's a man in the world who doesn't want to know and believe that he's a force to be reckoned with. We're all craving for someone to pay attention to our strength. And not just our physical strength. Sure, we want to feel strong physically, but it's so much more than that.

We want to know that we're *powerful*—that our words, our decisions, our presence have power and impact. And we want—we *need*—a man to point that out in us. Yes, we want our strength to provide a sense of safety, leadership, and impact for the women in our lives, but more than that we want men in our world to take note of our strength. We're competitive beasts, remember?

Surviving the Jungle

When I (Stephen) was a kid, the house next door had a huge, sloping lawn in the backyard. It started as a steep incline that gradually leveled out near the bottom. There was no fence, so the hill was open to all the other yards around it. In a neighborhood of small houses, this expanse of green was an oasis of freedom where the backyards of six or seven houses joined together. It became one of the main gathering spots for all the neighborhood kids to sled, logroll, ride bikes, and play the classic backyard game called King of the Hill.

The object of King of the Hill (also called King of the Mountain or King of the Castle) is to stay on top of a large hill or pile as "the king." Other players try to knock the current king off the hill, take his place, and thus become the new king. Reigns are often short lived.

The way kings can be toppled depends largely on the rules determined by the players before the game starts. In my neighborhood, this included pushing, pulling, and sometimes punching and kicking (or even biting, if that weird kid from around the corner showed up). King of the Hill was one of those games that taught us about life (whether we knew it or not). It was as close to jungle law as my suburban childhood got. It was survival of the fittest or fastest or smartest, or whoever was the last to be called home for supper. On those afternoons, between school and dinner, I learned more about how to use power playing King of the Hill than from anything my father ever taught me.

King of the Hill has become a familiar cultural metaphor for any sort of social activity in which a single person obtains power or status over multiple competitors, where winning can only be achieved by ousting the reigning champion. It's a lot like the reality TV show *Survivor*, whose slogan is "Outwit, Outplay, and Outlast." The rules of this next-gen game show are simple: A group of average Americans are abandoned in the middle of some unforgiving backwoods (such as Borneo, the Australian outback, Africa, a desert island, the Amazon, a Chinese forest) and divided into teams. They compete in challenges, and every few days the losing tribe must trek to a tribal council to vote out one of their own members.

Halfway through the game, the tribes merge into one, and the game changes to individual competitions with every man for himself. As the game shifts, players compete for "immunity" from being voted off that week. However, the players must be careful about who they send packing, because after the merging of the tribes, a jury of seven begins to form, and each week they return to watch the tribal council ceremony. At the end of the game, they vote for one of the members of the final two to win $1 million.

Survivor is a game of adaptation that focuses on the players and the social commentary that surrounds them. The game revolves around the question of how these players can "outwit, outplay, and outlast" each other. Really, it comes down to whoever is the most manipulative, controlling, sneaky, and powerful—in other words, whoever is the king of the hill.

Our culture defines leadership in much the same way as King of the Hill and *Survivor*. Whatever you need to do to get other people to do what you need them to do is fair game—within reason. But "reason" really depends on who is leading and in what culture the "game" is taking place. President Harry Truman said it this way: "My definition of a leader . . . is a man who can persuade people to do what they don't want to do, or do what they're too lazy to do, and like it."

So is that what leadership is? Is that what being a leader is all about—getting people to do what you want and make them like it? Though that may be one way of looking at it, we think that there is perhaps a bit more to it than that.

What Is a Leader?

At its most basic level, a leader is anyone who has power or position to guide, direct, or influence people. So, when we use the word *leader* in this chapter, we're not just talking about formal leadership roles; we're including all the relationships in which you have influence. Are you a leader at work? Maybe you are, but also consider leadership in terms of your marriage, parenting, friendships, in-laws, and extended family. Anywhere in this chapter where you see the word *leader,* you could insert *husband, father, friend,* and so on.

In most rock bands, the lead singer is the leader. Why? Is there something magical about the position? Not really. But the lead singer is the front man, the one who directs the show and is first to receive the acclaim and criticism. Most often, the lead singer is the one to whom everybody else looks and trusts to get the job done.[1] Rock stars, pastors, coaches, principals, fathers, husbands—you name it—use their influence to reach certain goals, and the goals are often more important to them than the people used in reaching them.

Too often, men assume their positions because of their desire to lead. Out of what are often legitimate passions and gifts, these leaders assume positions where they can more successfully exercise their will. They essentially lead in order to advance or promote the name of the organization, group, or entity they operate (whether that's a family, a business, a sports team, a church, or a civic organization). Their work is far more about performance (and getting others to perform) than it is about assistance. Being helpful or generous is secondary to landing on top.

But there's another leadership model out there too—a model that is all about helping others grow more fully into themselves and the expression of their giftedness.

This style does not focus primarily on production, but rather on people and how they thrive in the process. This alternate model of leadership is most commonly known as "servant leadership."

Would You Like Some Coffee with Your Dessert?

A servant leader is someone who takes an entirely different approach than someone who is a leader first. Becoming a servant leader begins with the desire to help—the desire to offer others the same comfort, compassion, and contentment that you as the leader have. Servant leadership says, "Someone profoundly helped me; and having received that gift, I now want to help others in the same way." A servant leader is a servant first, and the spirit of service is birthed out of passion and gratitude. Servant leadership is a decision that arises from a rescued heart, a reformed character, a reclaimed desire, and a renewed willingness. Because it is based on gratitude and rooted in a passion to serve, servant leadership becomes a way of being (rather than simply a role to be played). And though it may result in influence, authority, and power, servant leadership doesn't seek these things.

The difference between the two types of leaders (performance vs. service) couldn't be more stark. One is focused on production; the other is focused on people. Performance-based leadership is driven and directive, and it grows by promotion. Servant leadership is always reluctant and invitational, and it grows by attraction.

Servant leadership comes down to one main thing: caring to make sure that the people you serve are tended to. A servant leader is one who desires to give good to others for the others' good.[2] When it comes right down to it, we are designed to serve.[3] It is in the practice of service that our hearts are exposed and gratified. Nothing fills us as satisfyingly and completely as doing good on behalf of another.

God's Character

Service isn't only a way for us to *live out* how we are made; it's also a context for expressing God's character within us. The Bible paints a picture of a God who serves his people's greater good. And as his image bearers, we are made to do the same. Right from the beginning, in the Garden of Eden, we get a glimpse of our servant-oriented design: "The LORD God took the man and put him in the Garden of Eden to work it and take care of it."[4]

The phrase "work it and take care of it" is really instructive for us if we understand it from a Jewish perspective. The Hebrew word for "work," *abad*, more liter-

HOW TO SKIN A DEER

If you've got issues with hunting, feel free to move along to the next page. It's not our place to say whether you should or shouldn't hunt. We're just here to tell you how to skin a deer, in case you should happen to kill one.

1. Put your rifle back in the closet. Go get your hunting license and take a hunter's safety course offered by the state or local wildlife agency.

2. Once you're legal and educated, find something bright orange to wear, get your rifle or bow, and head out to the woods. (If you have a problem with hunting, you can just drive up and down the highway, looking for some fresh roadkill.)

3. Shoot a big buck.

4. Once your deer is dead, you're ready to field dress it. With a *very* sharp knife, cut from the genitals through the rib cage up to the sternum. Be careful to only cut through the skin and stomach muscle, and not too deep. You don't want to puncture anything in the digestive system.

5. Turn the deer on its side and allow the guts to fall out. You will need to cut away the fat that holds the intestines in. You will also need to pull the heart and lungs out with your hands. (The rest of the intestines should come along too.)

6. Wash up and get ready for some physical activity. Drag the deer out to the truck. Either load it in the back or strap it to the hood (if you're driving a car). Drive home or back to camp to do the skinning.

7. When skinning a deer, the carcass can either be hung head up or head down. Begin by making a circular cut around the deer's neck. Connect this cut with the cut made in the stomach during field dressing. Remove the hide by grasping the skin and pulling down hard with both hands. Use your knife carefully when freeing the hide from the carcass to avoid cutting the skin. If the flesh begins to pull off with the skin, stop pulling and try again after cutting the flesh back with your knife. (Note: You will need to cut off the front and hind leg bones from around the deer's knees with a hacksaw.)

8. By now, you are exhausted from getting up before dawn, driving out to the middle of nowhere, sitting for hours in a blind waiting for a deer to wander by, field dressing the deer and dragging it out of the woods, and skinning it. But you're not finished yet. You still need to store the meat for butchering.

9. First, cut the back strap and tenderloins out and place them in an ice chest. Next, cut the front legs free and place them in an ice chest. Cut the back hindquarters free by working your way to the ball-and-socket joint that holds the hindquarters to the hips. Work the knifepoint into this joint and work around the ball. Once both ten-dons are cut, the hindquarters will be free. Place any other meat, such as the ribs and the neck, into an ice chest. Pack the meat generously with ice and take the meat to the processor for butchering.

Adapted from the Maine Hunting & Fishing Camp Web site: http://maine-hunting-camp. com/fielddressingdeer.html.

ally means "to work for another" or "to serve another."[5] And the rest of the phrase, "to take care of it," comes from the Hebrew word *shamar*, which means "to keep guard" or "observe." So, from a biblical perspective, our work is meant to resemble that of a steward or a janitor—a servant—more than a CEO.

We were made by God to serve him and his creation by guarding, shaping, and nurturing what he made and what he gave us. We are here to serve each other. In living this out, we become servant leaders. People are drawn to us and trust us and are willing to follow in our footsteps.

How Are We to Lead?

Servant leaders fight for what's right, not for what's easy. They fight for lost causes—which some would say are the only causes really worth fighting for. Fighting for lost causes is the theme of Frank Capra's classic movie *Mr. Smith Goes to Washington*, in which we see a compelling picture of what it means to live as a servant leader.

Mr. Smith is the story of an idealistic and naive Midwesterner, Jefferson Smith (played by Jimmy Stewart), appointed to the U.S. Senate to fill in for an ailing senator. Upon arrival in the capital, Smith is reunited with the state's senior senator, his childhood hero Senator

Joseph Paine, who has presidential aspirations. But it's not long before Smith's eyes are opened to the seamier side of politics and the corruption of his hero, who is in league with the evil state political boss, Jim Taylor. Taylor first tries to corrupt Smith, then later attempts to destroy him through a scandal.

Fighting this lost cause, Smith finds himself filibustering the Senate. Everything is against him—his own inexperience, the power of Washington (embodied in Senator Paine), and the crooked media mogul Jim Taylor. In spite of the odds, Smith stands up and tells the truth. More than telling the truth, he risks his own reputation and invites the nation to a noble vision of who and what they were made to be. After hours of speaking, Smith, with his voice very hoarse and his legs very weak, makes one last thrust:

> Just get up off the ground, that's all I ask. Get up there with that lady that's up on top of this Capitol dome, that lady that stands for liberty. Take a look at this country through her eyes if you really want to see something. And you won't just see scenery; you'll see the whole parade of what Man's carved out for himself, after centuries of fighting.

Fighting for something better than just
jungle law, fighting so's he can stand
on his own two feet, free and decent,
like he was created, no matter what his
race, color, or creed. That's what you'd
see. There's no place out there for
graft, or greed, or lies, or compromise
with human liberties. And, if that's
what the grown-ups have done with
this world that was given to them,
then we'd better get those boys' camps
started fast and see what the kids can
do. And it's not too late, because this
country is bigger than the Taylors, or
you, or me, or anything else. Great
principles don't get lost once they
come to light. They're right here; you
just have to see them again![6]

Smith goes on to explain how to make this vision possible:

Because of just one, plain, simple
rule: Love thy neighbor. And in this
world today, full of hatred, a man who
knows that one rule has a great trust.

You know that rule, Mr. Paine, and I
loved you for it, just as my father did.
And you know that you fight for the
lost causes harder than for any others.
Yes, you even die for them.[7]

Smith's words echo a passage in the Bible that speaks to
the very issue of putting one's life on the line to defend
a worthy cause. In speaking of himself as the Good
Shepherd, Jesus draws a distinction between a shepherd
and a hired hand.

"I am the good shepherd. The good
shepherd lays down his life for the
sheep. The hired hand is not the
shepherd who owns the sheep. So
when he sees the wolf coming, he
abandons the sheep and runs away.
Then the wolf attacks the flock and
scatters it. The man runs away because
he is a hired hand and cares nothing
for the sheep."[8]

This passage illustrates how a shepherd has a passion for
the sheep and a willingness to lay his life down for those
he loves. On the flip side, the hired hand is unwilling to

become invested—unwilling to face up to the dangers that threaten the sheep—and thus is unwilling to truly love the people under his care.

It seems that the Judeo-Christian perspective of leadership is really quite different from any other. Not only is it servant leadership, but there's something about the kinds of leaders God chooses that is worth noting as well. Time and again in Scripture, when God chooses someone to lead, the person is unlike anything we might expect a qualified leader to be. More often than not, they are reluctant, inexperienced, lacking self-confidence, or thwarted by their own sin. Typically, they either lack vision or are ill-equipped to communicate it.

Like Capra's Jefferson Smith, leaders in the Bible tend to be people who would be unlikely to ever get elected to public office, run a Fortune 500 company, or be on the leadership team at a local church. In the Bible, we see leaders like

- Noah, who tended to drink too much;[9]
- Abraham, who likely worshiped other gods before God chose him;[10]
- Moses, who was hot tempered and lacked self-confidence in his leading;[11]
- Gideon, who openly complained about how God was doing things;[12]

- David, who became an adulterer, murderer, and liar;[13]
- Paul, who orchestrated genocide;[14]

Looking at all these examples, we begin to see that God does not choose leaders for any reason other than he wants to. He chooses small people and uses them for big things.

> Brothers, think of what you were when you were called. Not many of you were wise by human standards; not many were influential; not many were of noble birth. But God chose the foolish things of the world to shame the wise; God chose the weak things of the world to shame the strong. He chose the lowly things of this world and the despised things— and the things that are not—to nullify the things that are, so that no one may boast before him. It is because of him that you are in Christ Jesus, who has become for us wisdom from God—that is, our righteousness, holiness and redemption. Therefore, as it

> is written: "Let him who boasts boast
> in the Lord."[15]

Jesus was a leader in the same vein as other leaders in the biblical narrative. Looking at him in terms of modern-day leadership practices, he was not your typical "dress for success" kind of leader. He was reluctant (his mother had to encourage him to start his ministry).[16] He was a poor guy from the country, with few connections.[17] He had a spotty family tree (his lineage included murderers, adulterers, harlots, and non-Jews).[18] People often couldn't understand what he was saying through his parables and poetry.[19] He didn't seem to work very hard, spending a lot of time having dinner and taking walks by himself. And he was an ineffective networker, hanging out with people with really poor reputations.

But how he chose to lead was extraordinary. He was the consummate servant leader, weaving humility, bravery, and forgiveness into everything he did. If we want to have success in the art of servant leadership, this Jesus guy is a pretty good example to follow. He expressed his leadership in three primary ways: as prophet, priest, and king. Understanding these three expressions of servant leadership will help us to serve those we lead (or lead those we serve) well.

Prophet

In a biblical/historical context, the prophet is God's mouthpiece to call God's people to responsibility, repentance, and reconciliation. Prophets address current social, economic, and relational issues and provide a road map for restoration and transformation. In the Bible, these guys are responsible for proclaiming the word of the Lord.

Huh?

In regular, everyday English, these guys were the vision casters. In the biblical context, prophets did not so much predict the future as they did paint a picture of who God is, who we are, and how we can be reconciled and reunited with God. Jesus was the ultimate vision caster for God's plan, purposes, and programs.

The art of servant leadership invites us to be leaders whose hearts are directed by a vision for those we are called to serve. A vision is something we've seen, but it's also something we've been given. You know you're beginning to capture the essence of vision casting when the dreams you have for those you serve cause you to ache for what *could be*. The vision is always bigger than the leader; therefore, vision casting brings a sense of powerlessness and insufficiency.

In the Bible, one prophet describes the yearning like

this: His lips quivered, decay crept into his bones, and his legs trembled.[20] The risk of the servant leader is that they might cast a vision so big and so personal for those they serve that people will hate them or think they are foolish.

The vision that burned in the heart of Jesus was complete reconciliation between God and his creation. He saw how distant we are from God and was compelled to dream and speak of how things could be.

You know that you're casting a servant-leader-type vision if the people around you want to erase the picture you paint or judge it as unreasonable, impractical, or illogical. You know you're doing a really good job of vision casting when you're calling people to become all that God intended for them to be, and instead they come to hate you and want to kill you. Without a doubt, prophetic servant leadership requires bravery and a sure-footed sense of hope.

Priest

The second role of a servant leader is that of priest. The role of the priest in the history of Israel was to administer the law. As such, the priest was responsible for three things: guarding and interpreting the law; teaching people about the covenant between God and themselves; and administering the necessary rituals, sacraments, and sacrifices on behalf of the people. In short, the priestly role is to facilitate the process of reconciliation and preserve the stories about it.

As a priest, the servant leader becomes a receptacle for the stories of his community. Stories provide context and make it easier for people to internalize values. Servant leaders know that stories help to transmit lessons and shape the memory and reality of those they lead. That's why Jesus spent so much time telling stories.

In the priestly role, servant leaders hear stories, tell stories, and help to interpret (reconcile) stories. For this reason, servant leaders must be able to tell the truth about their own stories so that they can identify the truth in others. And the parts they need to know the best are the ones about conflict and loss.

Conflict and loss are unavoidable aspects of leadership; therefore, as priests within a community, servant leaders are responsible for helping reconcile the conflict and loss of those they lead. A servant leader must be willing to experience pain alongside and on behalf of those he serves. As a priest, a servant leader must be prepared to walk through sorrow. This means that a servant leader must know the true tragedy of his own story and how that affects his relationships. In his priestly role, a servant leader will sacrifice his own agenda, profit, and well-being for the well-being of those he serves. The capacity of a servant leader to lead well depends on his ability and willingness to suffer on behalf of someone else.

Redemptive suffering is a central theme in Jesus' life story. As priest, he was willing to suffer so that others could have what they so desperately wanted—reconciliation with God. In his suffering, he facilitated forgiveness.

Servant leaders facilitate reconciliation by serving as a bridge between stories of the past and the present-day unfolding of God's continued faithfulness. By looking back and retelling the story of redemption, servant leaders bolster the faith of others in reconciliation. The central message of the servant leader as priest is that God can be trusted today because in the past he has done what he said he was going to do—and he is unchanging. It is through the lens of faith that servant leaders help those they serve know who they are, where they have been, and where they are going.

King

The third role of a servant leader is that of king. The role of a king in the history of Israel was a compromise that God allowed in response to Israel's rejection of him. It was a way for Israel, prior to the coming of the Messiah, to have a picture of God's advocacy.

As king, each servant leader has been granted a realm of creation to tend, nurture, shape, and maintain. How we do this reveals the condition of our hearts before God. Whatever our own little kingdom looks like is a pretty good representation of what is going on in our hearts. As king, the servant leader's job is to protect the vulnerable through two primary functions: confronting injustice and demonstrating mercy.

Injustice is seen anywhere power is misused. (Injustice is really just a nicer word for *abuse*.) As king, a servant leader must be actively working to protect the vulnerable from the misuses of power. A king must bring together his resources to guard his people. Likewise, a king must demonstrate concern for those in his care who are less powerful. Servant leadership demands that those in need be given the resources they need. The servant leader as king is a blending of strength and tenderness.

The nature of kingship is a love born out of humility. It's a desire to rule for the greater good. Being a servant leader means that in recognizing our own vulnerability and neediness, we become willing to stand up for others and give to those who are in need.

Jesus modeled for us the complete package of prophet, priest, and king. He was the perfect prophet, being himself the Word of God and proclaiming the vision of God's Kingdom. He was the ultimate priest, as he took the form of a suffering sacrifice, offering his life for the salvation of creation. And he was the ultimate benevolent king, expressing a perfect blend of strength and tenderness. Jesus' life is a complete incarnation of servant leadership—from washing his disciples' feet to proclaiming the upside-down nature of God's Kingdom (where the first will be last and the last will be first). Here's what he said about true servant leadership:

> You know that those who are regarded as rulers of the Gentiles lord it over them, and their high officials exercise authority over them. Not so with you. Instead, whoever wants to become great among you must be your servant, and whoever wants to be first must be slave of all. For even the Son of Man did not come to be served, but to serve, and to give his life as a ransom for many.[21]

Three Strands of Servant Leadership

There are three different threads that weave together to make the tapestry of servant leadership: humility, courage, and forgiveness.[22] The sharing of power comes as an

HOW TO THROW A BASEBALL

It's as important as driving a car. As essential as clipping your nails. As universal as . . . well, *baseball.* You just gotta know how to throw a baseball, whether you play the sport or not. So listen up.

1. Don't face your target with your shoulders square. Throwing like that will inevitably result in the classic comment, "He throws like a girl," at some point in your life. Instead, turn your body and shoulders a quarter turn so that your front shoulder and elbow (your glove side) point straight at the target. The ball and your glove will be together, about chest high.

2. With knees slightly bent, transfer your weight to your back foot (your throwing-hand side), lift your front foot slightly off the ground, and step directly toward your target. As you transfer your weight back, begin to move your throwing hand down and back to begin the throwing motion.

3. As you step forward, move your throwing arm up and back so that your arm is straight back from shoulder to elbow and your hand (with the ball in it) is cocked at about the same level as your ear.

4. Now throw the ball. As your arm comes forward, swivel your hips to bring them square to the target and transfer your weight to your front foot, coming down on the ball of your foot with your knee slightly bent. This motion will also cause your back foot to move from fully planted up onto the ball of your foot and your toes.

5. Bring your arm over the top and release the ball out in front of your throwing shoulder as you plant your front foot. Throwing "over the top" increases strength, velocity, and accuracy. It also protects the arm from injury.

6. Let your forward momentum carry your back leg through until you are standing square to the target, with your glove ready to field the ball.

Now, play ball!

expression of all three working together. When one of these three is removed, the whole fabric unravels.

One thread, humility, can be understood as the experience we might have looking at the Alps or the Grand Canyon or out of an airplane window. It's an encounter with something so beautiful, majestic, and powerful that it leaves us slack-jawed. If only we could find the words to describe it.

Humility takes us to a place of confession and listening, in which we acknowledge our weaknesses and become open to receiving input from the people we lead.

In true humility, we can't help but see our weaknesses. But that's what keeps us dependent on the power of God as we rely on his strength. Let's face it—every leader carries some level of incompetence. But too often, as leaders, we try to hide, ignore, spin, manage, compensate, or strategize around our weaknesses, rather than embracing them. It's impossible to serve well when our energy is spent trying to cover up and manage our shortcomings.

But what does it mean to "embrace" our weaknesses?

If we hope to serve well, we must acknowledge our weaknesses and blunders (that is, admit them to ourselves) and name them out loud to those we serve. Admittedly, exposing one's own incompetence is hard for many leaders. But this is the only work that will transform our character and provide us a platform on which to build genuine respect and legitimate power.

But we must do more than simply expose and acknowledge our shortcomings; we must also dismantle them in front of the people we lead. As we confront our weaknesses, we become open to the impact they have on other people. We are no longer closed off to seeing how our actions affect others and how our style of leadership limits their ability to express themselves.

Instead of directors, we become listeners. Listening, which includes empathy, curiosity, and awareness, is a foundational practice of servant leadership. Almost everything else a servant leader can accomplish flows out of a commitment to listen carefully to what others have to say.

Leading with humility takes courage. To live humbly before those we are called to lead is a scary proposition. Admitting our own mistakes and weaknesses exposes us to the possibility of criticism, distrust, and isolation. It's like saying, "Hey, I'm a goofball and a screwup. I'm not really sure of everything I'm doing, and I know I really messed it up last time, and that it hurt you, but I'm kind of thinking we need to do *this*. You want to come along and help out?"

Admitting our mistakes will immediately expose our

greater character defects and our need for other people's help. Humble and courageous leaders are also dependent leaders.

The art of servant leadership requires that we give power away. In his book *Leading with a Limp*, Dan Allender describes how authentic leaders use their own power to make sure power is used fairly. Servant leaders shun pride and ambition and find joy in helping others achieve their goals and dreams. Giving up power doesn't mean we put on a false humility and thereby abdicate our gifts, authority, and experience; it means that we empower the ones we're leading so that they can step into and exercise their own gifts, authority, and experience.

Giving up power can be a scary proposition, and it requires a whole lot of courage for most leaders. But a servant leader is only as effective as his willingness to suffer and sacrifice on behalf of others. It takes courage because, when a servant leader is leading well, he will inevitably end up getting hurt. When he gives his heart in humility to the care of those around him, he's almost guaranteed to experience the sting of betrayal, the shame of mockery, or the loneliness of abandonment. In his passion to serve, he will almost always be harmed, because the very people for whom he is fighting will resist, disregard, or sabotage the process.

Conflict is a part of all relationships, and much of the work of leadership involves navigating the waters of conflict. Sometimes, conflict is friendly and constructive, and other times it is hostile and destructive. The pain of conflict takes its toll on relationships, and in the process a leader and those he serves can become hurt, angry, sad, afraid, and ashamed.

This is why forgiveness is such an essential thread in the tapestry of servant leadership. If a leader is unwilling to offer forgiveness to and seek forgiveness from those he is committed to serve, he will begin to carry resentments. Bitterness undermines relationship because it erodes the vital foundation of trust. The most humble and brave thing a leader can do is not just openly clean up his messes and share power with others. The most humble and brave thing a leader can do is forgive others for the mistakes they've made and seek forgiveness for his own.

To lead well, we must forgive, but forgiveness requires the courage to risk and the humility to recognize our own mistakes and transgressions. In forgiveness, we recognize the way things really are, complete with all the hurt, dysfunction, anger, and contempt, and we risk moving beyond our current circumstances and not carrying the past into the future. At its core, forgiveness is the willingness to cancel a debt in order to open a door for restoration.

Without forgiveness, a leader's vision becomes clouded by past events, and his capacity to hope and to cast vision evaporates. Without forgiveness, there is no future, only a constant rehashing of the past. That's why forgiveness is often the mechanism that unleashes the talent and energy of those being led to realize their potential. Forgiveness restores trust and allows people the freedom to risk being more of who they are—more genuine and open.

When humility, courage, and forgiveness are part of the leadership equation, everyone is propelled toward maximum service for others—both the leader and those being led. Servant leadership begins to break down the separations and stratifications of hierarchy. Leaders and followers alike begin to encounter each other as equals; they possess a deep mutual respect; they develop a sense of trust and community; and they mutually share decision-making power in appropriate ways.[23]

Calling Out Strength

Too many boys are thwarted on their way to becoming servant leaders because they are never properly initiated into manhood. When a father neglects or fails to deliberately and intentionally help his son navigate the passage from boyhood to manhood, the boy often gets stuck at a juvenile or transitional stage, which undermines his emotional and spiritual development. He may have the smarts and the savvy to act like a man—and, in fact, he is a man, with all the roles and responsibilities—but inside he still feels like a kid.

One of the most positive means of calling out a boy's strength is through the art of *initiation*. I (David) talk a lot with men and fathers about the importance of initiation in the life of a boy. Fortunately, quite a bit has been written on the subject. Guys like Robert Lewis, Michael Gurian, John Eldredge, Richard Rohr, and Donald Miller have spoken well to the lost art of male initiation. Initiation is quite simply the practice of a community of men ushering a boy into manhood.

Throughout most of human history, societies have had ceremonies, traditions, and rituals to create for boys a sense of being led into a sacred community of men. These practices are still alive and well in some cultures (for example, the Jewish bar mitzvah or the Native American tribal experience), but in most of twenty-first-century America, male initiation is a lost art. We've somehow lost our understanding of and appreciation for the value of this rich and vital rite of passage.

When fathers don't deliberately initiate their sons into manhood, the boys find their own rites of passage.

Having sex with a girl, joining a gang, stealing, speeding, smoking, jumping off a cliff, experimenting with drugs or alcohol—one way or another, young men will look for ways to validate their sense of manhood. We set our sons up for tragedy, failure, and heartbreak when we don't provide them with what they so desperately need and long to have; that is, a proper initiation into a community of men. Every young man hungers to have at least one older man take enough interest in him to discover his heart, explore his passions, and call out his masculine strength. Every young man needs at least one other man to lead him and instruct him in the ways of manhood. Male initiation changes the way a boy sees himself, his calling, his purpose, and his place in the world.

Jesus had a rite of passage as he began his earthly ministry. The Gospel of Matthew recalls a moment during the symbolic ritual of baptism, when God spoke his blessing on his Son: "This is my Son, whom I love; with him I am well pleased."[24] From there, Jesus went into the desert to be tested. Many Native American cultures have a similar wilderness experience as part of their manhood-initiation rites.

Initiation is a core component of servant leadership. It is the calling out of strength and the instruction in the responsible exercise of that strength. The Bible reminds us that "sons are a heritage from the LORD, children a reward from him. Like arrows in the hands of a warrior are sons born in one's youth. Blessed is the man whose quiver is full of them. They will not be put to shame when they contend with their enemies in the gate."[25]

Boys are like arrows in the hands of a warrior. An arrow in the hands of a warrior has the potential for great destruction and harm, but it also has the power for protection. Likewise, boys have potential for great destruction and harm, if left to their own devices. Masculine strength without wisdom, precision, and leadership isn't strength at all; it's just raw power. As adult men, our calling is to be intentional with our sons and to instruct them with attention, intention, and precision.

Too many men in our culture abuse their power because they never learned to harness it properly. The abuse of power isn't leadership at all—it's simply recklessness. Too many Christian men have abused their power and done so in the name of God. They have justified the exercise of power over others without attention to their true calling—the calling we have as husbands, fathers, and friends to love other people and lay down our lives as Christ did for his bride, the church. That is the art of servant leadership.

I (David) am so thankful to have grown up with a

dad who modeled servant leadership for me. He lived it out in the way he responded to his coworkers and colleagues. As I mentioned before, I've met countless individuals who worked for and alongside my father who speak of him with respect and honor. I well remember walking the halls of my dad's office and hearing him call out to everyone he encountered—whether it was the women and men who cleaned the building, a secretary, or a professor. He knew them all by name, and he often knew details of their lives.

My dad lived out the art of servant leadership at home, as well. My parents shared all responsibilities in the home. It wasn't uncommon to see my father preparing a meal or cleaning up afterward. There weren't archaic, rigidly defined roles under our roof. Equally so, the manner in which he interacted with my mother well illustrated this style of leadership. I never questioned that he cherished, celebrated, and honored my mom. Even in their conflict, I sensed his respect and care for her. My dad fought *for* my mother more than he fought *against* her.

Servant leadership differs from other styles of leadership by shunning a top-down style, instead emphasizing humility, courage, and forgiveness. At its heart, servant leadership requires that we make a conscious effort to serve better—not because we desire power, but because we long for others to realize their God-given potential in Christ.

Lessons Learned

1. Men crave power.
2. There are two types of leadership.
3. There are three strands in servant leadership.
4. Initiation is really important.

How to Move On from Here

Make a list of two to three men who have affected your life for good—men who acknowledged and affirmed your strength. Write them a letter or send an e-mail acknowledging their impact on your life.

Define your personal style of leadership (at work and at home). Identify your strengths and weaknesses. Make adjustments to bring your style into alignment with the principles of servant leadership. What needs to change? What needs to be affirmed? Take a risk and work with some other men to do this exercise. Don't settle for "accountability." Move beyond the checklist toward collaboration, vulnerability, and honesty. Practice with each other the central threads of servant leadership: humility, courage, and forgiveness. Read *Leading with a Limp*, by Dan Allender, and apply the wisdom you find there.

If you have a son, consider how you can create a rite of passage ceremony in his honor. For help with this, see *Raising a Modern-Day Knight*, by Robert Lewis; *Adam's Return: The Five Promises of Male Initiation*, by Richard Rohr; and *The Way of the Wild Heart: A Map for the Masculine Journey*, by John Eldredge. If you don't have a son, come alongside your friends who do and help them with the important responsibility of initiating their boys into manhood.

Conclusion

The Art of Grilling

I (David) am surrounded by a bunch of men who are masters at the art of grilling. My dad is the Tiger Woods of grilling steaks. I, on the other hand, am merely an adequate griller. You would never have the best steak you've ever put in your mouth at my table, but I could grill you a tasty burger, or at least help you avoid salmonella.

In addition to my dad, my father-in-law is exceptional at grilling. He has special grilling tools, fancy flavored briquettes, and a very expensive temperature gauge that measures the temp of the meat in all layers. It's extremely intimidating to stand around the Weber with him.

He lives in Florida, so we don't get the "opportunity" to grill together very often. But once a year, my family vacations together with my wife's parents, her brother and his wife, and their four kids at a beautiful place on Marco Island. The place where we stay has a ten-foot-long grill outside, where grillers of every stripe can attend to fresh fish, filet mignon, or their choice of delicacy. It has become an evening ritual for the men to gather around the grill to prepare the main course for dinner, talk about sports and work, and simply stand around together, the way men do.

This past year, there was a true grillmaster and self-proclaimed philosopher vacationing the same week we were at Marco. We'll call him Sirloin Yoda. Sirloin Yoda looked to be in his mid-fifties, and he was pushing 275 pounds, easy. (There's no question this guy had gnawed on his fair share of T-bones.) He and I developed a relationship during the nightly grilling ritual, and he would freely share his thoughts on grilling and life. He said things like, "Women are like a fine piece of steak. They're expensive and require a boatload of time, attention, and nurture. They're either flaming hot or ice cold, and rarely anything in between. Some women, like steaks, are prime cuts, and others are, well, . . . others."

Honestly, he would go on like this for a good hour or so each evening. In addition to the "life lessons" he offered, he instructed us all on seasonings, grilling fresh fish, basting the grill with olive oil, when to flip the meat, and everything else you never dreamed you didn't know about grilling.

On night three of our vacation, my father-in-law announced that he needed to make a work call and would leave the night's grilling to me. This meant I would be responsible for feeding the entire family. I felt a sense of panic race up one side of me and down the other. I prayed that Sirloin Yoda would not be taking the night off and would instruct me—as he had so willingly on previous nights. When I arrived at the downstairs grill, Yoda was nowhere to be found. I stood paralyzed, staring at the long expanse of grill. Finally, I decided to light the darn thing. I had a plate full of marinated chicken and two rooms full of hungry people waiting on me to come through.

I had just placed the last piece onto the grill when I heard a familiar voice approaching me from behind. I turned, and it took everything in me not to yell, "You're here, Jedi Master. Instruct me, O great one." My face must've said it all, because Sirloin Yoda immediately took to instructing me. "Turn down the flame. That marinade is oil based, isn't it? That'll cause your flames to rise and burn the outside, leaving the interior undone. Next time, I want you to skin that chicken."

I immediately turned down the flame and listened for further instructions. At one point in the exchange, Yoda grabbed the tongs from me and started poking and flipping on his own. I backed away and let him work his magic. He was spouting off about the war in Iraq and the government's response. He moved back and forth, teasing the meat to perfection as he pontificated. It was like watching an intense, passionate, and demanding conductor leading an orchestra. The flames rising and falling. Chrome tongs and spatulas waving. Herbs and seasonings flying everywhere. Periodically, I nodded and affirmed the symphony, but I was merely a spectator. The smell was intoxicating, and I was readying myself to take full credit when I presented to the family a heaping platter of chicken, grilled to perfection. No one would ever have to know that Sirloin Yoda was a poultry master as well. (The only problem was that the chicken would taste so good that everyone would know I'd had little to do with it.)

I couldn't stop thinking about the scene from *She's Having a Baby*, a John Hughes film from the late 1980s, when Jake Briggs (played by Kevin Bacon) makes his debut at the grill. He and his wife, Kristy (Elizabeth McGovern), have recently settled into a new three-bedroom, two-bath house in suburbia. They've invited both sets of parents over to admire (and critique) their attempt at domesticity. The scene opens with a view of the new house and smoke pouring out from the backyard. The camera zooms in on Jake, in a button-down shirt and cardigan, as he's working the grill. The fire is roaring, and as Jake flips a steak, it falls unceremoniously to the ground. He picks up the charred piece of meat, now covered with dirt, and looks around to see if anyone has witnessed the accident. Realizing he's in the clear, he immediately shakes the excess dirt and grass clippings from the slab of beef and tosses it back on the grill in an attempt to eliminate any further evidence of his error.

The following scene opens with everyone seated around the table. Jake is seated at one end of the table with Kristy at the other. Their parents are seated on either side. Jake has a look of exhaustion and dread pasted across his face as he munches on chips and avoids his steak. The only sound is that of all four parents struggling to saw away at their rubbery slabs of meat. Meanwhile, Kristy is making every effort to lighten the mood, but soon her father decides to offer Jake some feedback.

> **Father-in-Law:** This is good, Jake. You're quite a barbeque chef. What fascinates me is how you got it blood raw on one side and charred to a crisp on the other.
>
> **Jake's Dad:** Well, my steak's just fine, Russ.
>
> **Jake's Mom:** Mine, too, darling.
>
> **Father-in-Law:** What is this? (He scrapes

off a dark substance from the underside of the steak). Is this dirt on here?

(He continues scraping and then pauses to look at Jake).

Father-in-Law: Did you say something, Jake?

Jake (looking clueless): No, no.[1]

What guy hasn't been caught in some version of this scene? Caught in the attempt to look competent in the eyes of people whose respect he longs for, yet exposed by evidence that he doesn't have a clue.

At times, we've experienced Jake's plight because no one gave us any instruction. We never got our hands on the manual. Or maybe we got some of the information but were still left to stumble our way through on the journey to manhood. Whatever our particular stories, we're all prone to fumbling the ball.

Looking for the Right Playbook

In an effort not to mess up the game, many guys set out looking for the right playbook. At churches across the country, men get together in large and small groups to address the question of what it means to be a "real man." At my (Stephen's) church, we offer a class on Wednesday mornings. By many measures, these groups have turned out to be very successful ministries, drawing thousands of men into a deeper faith; equipping them to love God, family, and friends more fully; and providing a much-needed masculine context for fellowship and relationship. Much of the material covered in these sessions offers wisdom and is helpful to men to some degree.

But here's the problem: Most of the guys who participate in these groups are looking for solutions and tools that will help them master something that cannot be mastered. They come looking for a program and a promise that if they'll just apply themselves diligently enough, they can gain control of their lives and avert a crisis.

But that's just not true. It's not real life. It's not how God set the table. The system is broken, and no amount of diligence in keeping a program is going to change it. Authentic manhood has nothing to do with *performance* and everything to do with *presence*. It's not *what* we do or *how well* we do it; it's more a question of whether we're *showing up* in our day-to-day lives. Do we bring everything we have to the process of our lives?

Often, several weeks into the class, guys start calling my office wanting help. They are buried under the weight of immense shame and guilt. They've tried their hardest to be "a real man," and it's not working for them. With all the self-will they can muster, they've rejected whatever passivity they could identify, accepted far too much responsibility for everyone else, led so courageously that they have ended up alone, and placed a lot of expectations on God to reward their efforts.

The lucky ones ask for help when they're humiliated but not yet broken. (The unlucky ones keep trying harder and harder.) They come asking for the playbook on how to apply the laws of manhood that seem to be working for everybody else but aren't working for them. Like one guy I met with a few months ago after his teenage son was arrested. He said to me, "I've read all the books, faithfully attended four years of the men's class, committed two years of my life to a small-group Bible study for men, gone to Colorado for retreats three times, taken my kids camping and my wife to marriage conferences. I've done it all. But it's like the more I try to get this figured out, the worse I am at it."

Everywhere we turn, guys are saying the same kinds of things to us. They're stumbling through adulthood, trying to get it all together (or worse, *pretending* they have it all together). Much of their energy and self-image is tied to how well they can hide their problems and cluelessness.

But here's an important bit of news: There is no play-book to memorize. There is no one-size-fits-all solution to manhood. We're never going to "get it right" and then be able to kick back in the La-Z-Boy and put our feet up. What we have instead is a mess (called life), a story, a solution, and the challenge of taking what we have and finding something that reflects what God intends for us as men made in his image.

Hear us well. It's not about making the best with what you've been given. It's about first *recognizing* what you've been given. Then it's about *seeing* the One who gave it to you. And finally, it's about the process of *yielding* what you've been given back to the One who gave it to you in the first place.

It's not about performing or overachieving or mas-tering. It's about the process of learning to live in the freedom of knowing that it's not up to you to do any-thing.

It's about God.

It's about having the courage *not* to pick up the ball after you've dropped it. It's about growing in your willingness to let God take care of the ball. It's about understanding that God has *already* provided (through Jesus) a solution—not just for eternity, but also for *every day*.

HOW TO GRILL A GREAT STEAK

Good friends, outdoor music, a nice summer breeze, cold drinks, a hot fire, and meat—all the ingredients for a perfect July backyard cookout. And the centerpiece of the occasion is the grill. (For those on the West Coast, it's not called a *barbecue*. Barbecue's a Southern specialty involving pork, smoke, spices, and time.) Though it's easier and cheaper to throw some frozen burgers or brats on the grill, real men eat steak (also known as warrior food). And if you're going to spring for steak, you may as well learn how to grill it. Great grilling requires attention to three key ingredients: the grill, the meat, and the cooking.

The Grill: Though a charcoal grill is preferable for the taste, smell, and ambiance it produces, novices will likely do better with a gas grill. It's easier, faster, and more forgiving. Size doesn't matter; a two-burner gas grill will do the job.

The Meat: The next step to grilling a perfect steak is your choice of the perfect cut of meat. With a few exceptions, the rib (rib eye), short loin (T-bones and New York strips), and sirloin cuts typically yield the best steaks. The tenderloin (or filet) is the most expensive and by far the most tender steak of all. The tenderloin sacrifices some flavor for its tenderness and contains a relatively small amount of marbling, meaning that if it is cooked beyond medium, it will end up being dry and tough.

Most meat sold in grocery stores is graded. The grading system basically looks at four things: color, texture, firmness, and the amount of marbling (fat woven through the flesh). The more marbling, the higher the grade. The grading system is divided into eight tiers, though most consumers are concerned with only the top five: Prime, Choice, Select, Standard, and Commercial. Prime is the best of the best but hard to find at the grocery store. (Most of it is sold to restaurants.) Choice is usually your best bet (and only a small step down from Prime.) Next comes Select, which isn't as "select" as it sounds. You'll start to notice a difference in flavor and tenderness here, so choose a steak graded at least Choice.

The steaks selected should be bright red, with nice, white fat and marbling. New York strips and rib eyes combine the best of both tenderness (filet) and flavor (sirloin). A good range for steak thickness is 1¼ inches to 2¼ inches.

The Cooking: A number of mistakes are made before the steak ever hits the grill. One common mistake made by many backyard grillers is to pull out the steaks, remove the grocery store plastic wrap, and immediately plop the meat on the grill. True grillmasters know that a steak needs to be brought to room temperature first to ensure proper cooking. This is also the time to season the meat. Generously season each side of the steak with salt and pepper. This will give the seasonings time to dissipate across the surface of the steak, resulting in a better-seasoned piece of meat.

Another common mistake is not allowing the grill to heat properly. If you're cooking with charcoal, you want a nice, even ash on your coals. If you're cooking with gas, you want an even flame and a hot grill.

Once the grill is ready, put the steaks directly over the coals or the flame, and then leave them alone. Don't touch, poke, prod, or otherwise play with your food. Don't flip it, check it, or press it. Let the steaks sit unmolested for three or four minutes. (They need that time for the sugars to start to caramelize and produce a flavorful crust.) After three or four minutes, turn the steak using tongs. (Poking it with a fork will spill the juices.) Wait another three or four minutes (depending on the thickness of your steaks) and flip 'em again. Keep a spray bottle of water with you at all times. Use it to douse flame-ups. Flames licking at your steaks will deposit carbon on them and give your steaks a bitter, off flavor.

How do you know when your steaks are done? You can tell by the way it feels. (Don't cut into your steaks, or you'll dry them out.) A rare steak will feel like the large, fleshy part of your hand (at the base of your thumb) when you bring your thumb and forefinger together. Now bring your thumb and middle finger together—that's medium. Well-done corresponds to the feel of your hand when you bring your thumb and pinky together. "Well-done" is a terrible state of existence for a steak. Medium rare to medium is really the perfect temperature. With their relatively low fat content, steaks cooked beyond medium start to get tough and dry.

The final and most important step is to allow the steaks to "rest" or "heal" before you serve them. Remove the meat from the grill and allow it to sit for five minutes so the juices can disperse throughout the steak again. Without this time to rest, all the juices will flow out onto your plate when you cut into the steak, instead of staying where they belong, in the meat.

Adapted from Peter Martin, "Grilling the Perfect Steak," www.cheftalk.com/content/display. cfm?articleid=214, and www.cheftalk.com/content/display.cfm?articleid=215&type=article; and Gillian Duffy, "How to Grill the Perfect Steak," http://nymag.com/nymetro/food/homeent/ features/676.

Hot off the Grill

When it comes to successful grilling, it's less about hard-and-fast rules and more about paying attention to certain basic principles. The same is true of life. Likewise, both the art of life and the art of grilling involve the ability to adapt to changing circumstances and paying attention to what's going on around us without being distracted by unnecessary things. We may feel confident as we step out into the world, or we may feel as if we don't have what it takes. Either way, there are some things that we all need to understand (and pass along to our sons) if we (and they) are going to live authentically.

We need to understand that the world is a wicked place under the control of evil. We need to recognize that forces of good and evil are at war, and we need to choose a side. We need to know that neutrality is a vote for evil.

We need to know that we are forces to be reckoned with. We need to know that we have specific gifts, talents, and attributes that are powerful, creative, worthwhile, and valuable.

We need to know that we have specific shortcomings, character defects, and tendencies that are selfish, destructive, dangerous, and shameful.

We need to know that our words and actions have the power to bless and to curse—and we need to choose wisely.

We need to see that emotions belong in the lives of men, and we need to learn how to articulate our hearts.

We need to be at the center of the lives of at least one or two men that we love and respect. We need verbal affirmation and physical affection from these men—we need to be told and shown that we are loved by them.

We need a rite-of-passage experience. And we need to celebrate our victories.

We need to know how to cherish, respect, and honor women.

We need to know that life is not all about competition. We need to learn how to collaborate.

We need to learn how to grieve, because life is painful and full of loss.

We need to know that all of our needs won't be met by other people in our lives. And when we wake up to our unmet needs, we need to know that it is our responsibility, honor, and privilege to seek God to fulfill our needs.

Putting the Ball in Play

Every day is ripe with the possibility of failure and the reality of loss. The hard truth is that we can never escape this as long as we live east of Eden and west of Glory. No matter how many conferences we attend, Bible studies we do, books we read, or accountability partners we have, we cannot escape the reality of our predicament in this broken world. Life is full of pain, and the majority of the pain comes from the people we love. And no matter how hard we try as men, we will fail more than we succeed.

But that doesn't mean we can't be successful.

It's kind of like trying to hit a curveball. We're going to miss more often than not. But if we succeeded in getting a hit only 40 percent of the time, we'd be putting up Hall of Fame numbers on the baseball field, even while failing to get a hit 60 percent of the time. Did you know that the career record holder for on-base percentage (Ted Williams at .481) *failed to get on base more than 50 percent of the time*? Yet he is widely considered the greatest hitter ever to play the game.

In that way, baseball is a lot like life. It's a game of hard knocks, and the breaks don't always go our way. It's a game that requires perseverance and patience, skill and heart. It's a game full of failure and frustration—but also fantastic finishes. It's all about doing your best, every day, and then forgetting about the last game as you look forward to the next. To borrow a famous sports saying, it's not whether you win or lose;

it's not even so much how you play the game. What's important is that you're in the game—all the way in, with everything you've got. That's what it means to live an authentic life. That's how you were designed to play.

Okay, so let's come to grips with the fact that we didn't get everything we needed from our fathers. And let's admit to ourselves, and to others, that we're often ill-equipped and incompetent. But let's not stop there. Let's keep trying to hit that curveball called life, and let's show up every day ready to play—even to get thumped.

What would it look like for you to live fully—to be fully alive? And what would it take for you to pour what you have into the next generation? Every day, I (David) sit with boys who hunger for the men in their lives to pay more attention to them and to affirm the men they are becoming. I work with boys who are starving—literally famished in their souls—for that kind of attention. They can't get the sense of what it means to be a man from their mothers. But they can get it from you, and from me.

I'll never forget one Saturday morning when I was an early adolescent, standing in front of the bathroom mirror with my dad, a can of shaving cream, and a sink full of warm water. The memory is still vivid in my mind. My dad opened a black leather case and pulled out a chrome-handled razor from a kit of grooming tools. He opened a bottle of aftershave and invited me to smell it. Then he lathered up and carefully demonstrated the art of shaving—how to rinse every one to two strokes, the direction to move the blade, and how to avoid massacring my face. I might have had twelve facial hairs at most at the time, but my dad coached me with great care and respect in this sacred rite of passage. We shaved together, and as we did, we talked about how a man presents and carries himself in the company of others. We then graduated to a discussion of women. I recall my dad saying, "David, you should know that most women don't appreciate the feeling of a coarse beard against their skin when they kiss, so keep that in mind when you think about skipping a day of shaving."

Standing in front of the mirror that morning with my dad, I learned so much more than a handful of grooming techniques. I learned that the smell of aftershave is strong; that a woman loves to touch and kiss a smooth face; that you always feel like a man when you shave; and that a man's restraint is as potent as his strength. The information my dad gave me was meant to provide instruction, but more than that, it was designed to be a shared experience between father and son—sharing wisdom and experiencing relationship. When a dad does this well, his sons will never forget.

Dads, our sons long to feel our presence—physically, emotionally, and spiritually. They want to push up against us and feel their own strength as well as ours. There is much we don't have to offer them that we wish we did, but there's even more that we do have to offer. And that's the place we want to live from. That's how we want to take the lessons we've learned—and even the lessons our fathers didn't teach us—and make a positive difference in our own lives and in the lives of our sons and their sons after them. We won't do it perfectly, but we can do it with all our hearts.

Will you join us?

Notes

Introduction
1. Romans 8:18-27
2. Galatians 5:1
3. 1 Samuel 16:7
4. Erwin Raphael McManus, *Soul Cravings: An Exploration of the Human Spirit* (Nashville: Thomas Nelson, 2006), 3.

Chapter 1: How to Hit a Curveball
1. Donald Miller and John MacMurray, *To Own a Dragon: Reflections On Growing Up without a Father* (Colorado Springs: NavPress, 2006), 104–106.
2. Stu Weber, *Tender Warrior: Every Man's Purpose, Every Woman's Dream, Every Child's Hope* (Sisters, OR: Multnomah, 1999).
3. Psalm 8:3-5, NLT
4. Philippians 2:12

Chapter 2: Hide and Seek
1. Deuteronomy 4:9
2. Frederick Buechner, *Telling Secrets* (San Francisco: Harper, 1991), 33.

Chapter 3: Soft Curves and Softer Lips
1. Much of our understanding about the place of feelings in our lives, and their utmost importance as a way of more fully knowing and being ourselves, comes from the work of Dr. Chip Dodd, a friend and mentor of Stephen's, who runs a treatment center for impaired and addicted professionals in Nashville (www.cpe nashville.com). Chip has written a great book about the significance of feelings, called *The Voice of the Heart: A Call to Full Living* (Sage Hill Resources, 2001).
2. Harry W. Schaumburg, *False Intimacy: Understanding the Struggle of Sexual Addiction,* revised edition (Colorado Springs: NavPress, 1997), 17.
3. http://xxxchurch.com/gethelp/index.php.
4. C. S. Lewis, *A Grief Observed* (New York: HarperCollins, 1961), 38.

Chapter 4: Pop the Hood
1. Genesis 3:17-19
2. Many of these thoughts on shame are developed more fully in the work of Dr. Chip Dodd.
3. Matthew 5:22
4. James 5:16, NLT

Chapter 5: Bringin' Home the Bacon

1. *Say Anything* (20th Century Fox, 1989). Written and directed by Cameron Crowe.
2. James 2:26, NKJV
3. Genesis 2:7-9, 19
4. See Ephesians 1:9-14.
5. See Hebrews 11:40.
6. 2 Corinthians 6:1
7. Matthew 11:30, authors' paraphrase
8. Matthew 11:30
9. For a great picture of God's love, check out these two movies: *Babette's Feast* and *Antwone Fisher* (particularly the banquet scenes).
10. Genesis 3:17-19
11. *The Villages,* http://www.thevillages.com.
12. Ecclesiastes 1:2

Chapter 6: Pinewood Derby

1. "Pinewood Derby Model Car Racing," *U.S. Scouting Service Project,* www. usscouts.org/pinewood/cspine.asp
2. Isaac Minis Hays, *The Record of the Celebration of the Two Hundredth Anniversary of the Birth of Benjamin Franklin* (Philadelphia: American Philosophical Society, 1906), 90.

Chapter 7: King of the Hill

1. What's interesting is that this is not true for some of the most successful bands. So even though Bono, John Lennon, and Mick Jagger are the front men for U2, The Beatles, and The Rolling Stones, you can't really imagine those bands without The Edge, Paul McCartney, and Keith Richards.
2. According to Robert Greenleaf, who is credited with coining the phrase *servant leadership*, "the best test [of servant leadership] and difficult to administer is this: Do those served grow as persons; do they, *while being served*, become healthier, wiser, freer, more autonomous, more likely themselves to become servants?" ("The Servant as Leader" in *Servant Leadership* [Mahwah, NJ: Paulist, 1977], 27. Italics in original.) Greenleaf spent his first career—forty years—at AT&T before he retired in 1964 as director of management research. That same year, he founded the Center for Applied Ethics (later renamed the Greenleaf Center for Servant-Leadership). For another twenty-five years, he had an illustrious second career as an author, teacher, and consultant. Greenleaf, who died in 1990, was the author of numerous books and essays on the theme of servant leadership, including *Teacher as Servant* (1979) and *Servant Leadership* (1977), and three posthumous collections: *The Power of Servant Leadership* (1998), *On Becoming a Servant Leader* (1996), and *Seeker and Servant* (1996).

3. When it comes right down to it, we are all created to serve, but no one is created to be a slave. Slaves and servants are fundamentally different. No one is created to be subordinated. We all understand that we are made to be free and with worth. We all know deep within ourselves that what we learned in civics is true: Our freedom is "self-evident," and we all are created equal and gifted by God with certain nontransferable rights that we can't give away, trade in, or sell, even if we wanted to—things such as "life, liberty, and the pursuit of happiness."

4. Genesis 2:15

5. Incidentally, the related Arabic word means "to worship."

6. *Mr. Smith Goes to Washington* (Columbia, 1939). Written by Lewis R. Foster and Sidney Buchman. Directed by Frank Capra. The quote can be found online at www.imdb.com/Find?select=Quotes&for=Jefferson%20Smith.

7. Ibid.

8. John 10:11-13

9. See Genesis 9:20-21.

10. Joshua 24:2: "Joshua said to all the people, 'This is what the LORD, the God of Israel, says: "Long ago your forefathers, including Terah the father of Abraham and Nahor, lived beyond the River and worshiped other gods."'" Abraham grew up in a home that practiced idolatry.

11. See Exodus 2, 3, and 6; and Numbers 20, among others.

12. See Judges 6.

13. See 2 Samuel 11.

14. See Acts 9, 13:9.

15. 1 Corinthians 1:26-31

16. See John 2.

17. See Matthew 2.

18. Matthew 1

19. See Matthew 13.

20. See Habakkuk 3:16.

21. Mark 10:42-45

22. *Practicing Servant Leadership: Succeeding through Trust, Bravery and Forgiveness*, Larry C. Spears and Michele Lawrence, eds. (San Francisco: Jossey-Bass, 2004).

23. Much of the thinking behind these three concepts is adapted from the work being done at the Greenleaf Center. This secular think tank is an international, not-for-profit institution, headquartered in Indianapolis, founded to help people understand the principles and practices of servant leadership.

24. Matthew 3:17

25. Psalm 127:3-5

Conclusion

1. *She's Having a Baby* (Paramount, 1988). Written and directed by John Hughes.

About the Authors

Stephen James and David Thomas are coauthors of the companion books *"Does This Dress Make Me Look Fat?"* and *"Yup." "Nope." "Maybe."* (Tyndale), as well as *Becoming a Dad: A Spiritual, Emotional and Practical Guide* (Relevant). Stephen and David are regularly featured on radio and television, including ABC Family Channel's *Living the Life,* and in numerous publications, including *Discipleship Journal* and *Relevant* magazine.

Stephen is the congregational care pastor at Fellowship Bible Church in Brentwood, Tennessee. He speaks frequently about men's issues, marriage/relationships, and authentic spirituality. Stephen received his master's in counseling from Mars Hill Graduate School at Western Seminary, Seattle. He and his wife, Heather, live in Nashville with their four children.

David is director of counseling for men and boys at Daystar Counseling Ministries in Nashville. He and his wife, Connie, have a daughter and twin sons.

Also by Stephen James and David Thomas

Why won't he stop and ask for directions?

Is sex *all* he thinks about?

Are men just emotionally constipated?

Is he really as clueless as he acts?

"Yup." "Nope." "Maybe."

At long last, a woman's guide to getting more out of the language of men.

Now available in stores and online.

Also by Stephen James and David Thomas

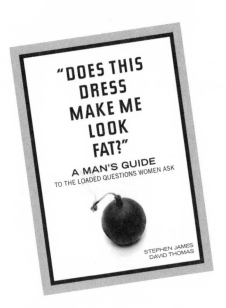

"Do you think that woman is pretty?"

"Is there anything you don't like about me?"

"What are you thinking about?"

"Does this dress make me look fat?"

Finally . . . a man's guide to the loaded questions women ask.

Now available in stores and online.